# Irrigation, Timber, and Hydropower

## Negotiating Natural Resource Development on the Flathead Indian Reservation, Montana, 1904-1945

# Irrigation, Timber, and Hydropower

**Negotiating Natural Resource Development on the Flathead Indian Reservation, Montana, 1904-1945**

by
**Garrit Voggesser**

published by
**Salish Kootenai College Press**
**Pablo, Montana**

distributed by
**University of Nebraska Press**
**Lincoln, Nebraska**

Cover design: Corky Clairmont, artist/graphic designer, Pablo, Montana. Cover illustrations: Chief Charlo, ca. 1910 (NA 8NS-75-97-221, box 7, 222), Flathead Irrigation Project Papers, U.S. National Archives, Denver Region, Denver, Colorado; Kerr Dam photo courtesy of David Rockwell, Dixon, Montana.

Text illustrations: Chapter 1: Flathead Irrigation Project Papers, U.S. National Archives, Denver Region, Denver, Colorado.
Chapter 3: Photographer Charles Owen Smithers, Smithers and Son Photography, Butte, Montana. Identifications courtesy of Felicite Sapiel McDonald.

Library of Congress Cataloging-in-Publication Data:
Names: Voggesser, Garrit, author.
Title: Irrigation, timber, and hydropower : negotiating natural resource development on the Flathead Indian Reservation, Montana, 1904-1945 / by Garrit Voggesser.
Other titles: Negotiating natural resource development on the Flathead Indian Reservation, Montana, 1904-1945
Description: Pablo, Montana : Salish Kootenai College Press, [2017] | Includes bibliographical references and index.
Identifiers: LCCN 2017040522 | ISBN 9781934594193 (pbk.)
Subjects: LCSH: Confederated Salish & Kootenai Tribes of the Flathead Reservation, Montana--Government relations. | Flathead Indian Reservation (Mont.)--Economic conditions--20th century. | Flathead Indian Reservation Irrigation and Power Project (U.S.)--History. | Kerr Dam (Mont.)--History. | Irrigation projects--Montana--History. | Water-power--Montana--Flathead Indian Reservation. | Water resources development--Montana--Flathead Indian Reservation. | Forests and forestry--Montana--Flathead Indian Reservation. | Forest products industry--Montana--Flathead Indian Reservation. | Flathead Indian Reservation (Mont.)--History--20th century.
Classification: LCC E99.S2 V64 2017 | DDC 978.6/033--dc23
LC record available at https://lccn.loc.gov/2017040522

Published by Salish Kootenai College Press, PO Box 70, Pablo, MT 59855. Distributed by University of Nebraska Press, 1111 Lincoln Mall, Lincoln, NE 68588-0630, order 1-800-755-1105, www.nebraskapress.unl.edu.

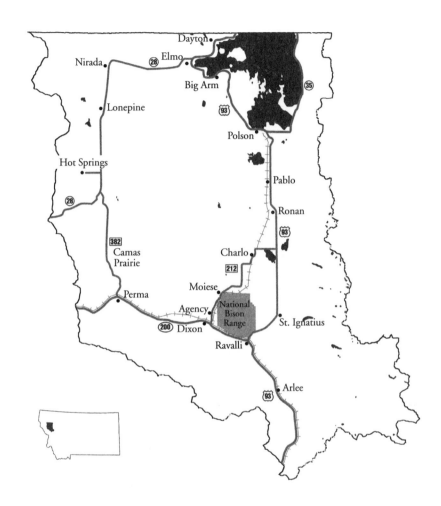

Flathead Indian Reservation, Montana

Map by Wyatt Design, Helena, Montana.

# Table of Contents

# Preface

## by Robert Bigart

The first half of the twentieth century was a time of continual onslaught on the natural resources of the Flathead Indian Reservation and the economic well-being of the tribal community. At the start of the century, then-Congressman Joseph M. Dixon moved a bill through the U.S. Congress, without tribal consent, to allot the Flathead Reservation and sell the "surplus" land to white settlers. The allotment led to the development of the Flathead Irrigation Project and later to the building of a hydropower dam at the foot of Flathead Lake. Garrit Voggesser's book describes the decades long battles as the tribes struggled to keep control of the land and water as off-reservation interests tried to appropriate the resources to benefit various non-Indian groups.

The manuscript included in this book was part of Voggesser's 2004 Ph.D. dissertation at the University of Oklahoma in Norman. The dissertation covered natural resource development in the Blackfeet and Fort Peck Reservations in addition to the Flathead Reservation. The full work was entitled, "Of Woods, Wilderness, and Water: Negotiating Natural Resources on the Blackfeet, Flathead, and Fort Peck Reservations, 1885-1945." Voggesser did an impressive amount of research for his dissertation. He examined a mountain of documentary sources, including various government archives, Congressional hearings, local newspapers, and a number of collections of private papers. The result is the first survey of natural resource development on the Flathead Indian Reservation during the first half of the twentieth century. The period covered by Voggesser's manuscript was a time of dramatic change on the reservation. In the twenty-first century, the tribes are still struggling to cope with some of the consequences of government actions between 1900 and 1950.

Much of Voggesser's information came from government archives and local newspapers, but these sources largely give the viewpoints of the government agencies and white settlers. Voggesser worked hard to include tribal viewpoints in his telling of the story, but only glimpses were preserved in the records he used. The conflicts between the Flathead Business

Committee and the Flathead Tribal Council over the use of tribal funds to construct the Flathead Irrigation Project and the efforts of Marie Lemery and the Flathead Tribal Council to reduce the reimbursable appropriations for the irrigation project in the 1910s are stories to be more fully told by a future researcher. Another topic to be explored would be the debates within the tribal community over these government policies, but this story is largely in the oral traditions of the tribal elders. The dramatic story in Voggesser's book tells an important part of Flathead Indian Reservation resource history, but it is not the entire story. Hopefully this book will motivate other researchers to record and preserve the oral history which will compliment and expand on the written records Voggesser used. Salish Kootenai College Press offers this book as a contribution to the history and current affairs of the Flathead Indian Reservation.

**************

For centuries before the first white men arrived in western Montana, the Bitterroot Salish, Upper Pend d'Oreille, and Lower Kootenai Indians lived well in the Northern Rocky Mountains and northwest Great Plains. The traditional tribal economies were centered on big game hunting, including seasonal buffalo hunts on the plains, and gathering the many wild berries and edible root crops in the area. In the eighteenth century, the arrival of the horse enabled a florescence of the tribal economy as the horse expanded tribal mobility, allowed the transport of larger cargos, and made hunting more productive. The Flathead Reservation tribes were engaged in long-term conflict with the expanding plains tribes such as the Blackfeet and Sioux. The western Montana tribes welcomed the arrival of white traders and missionaries as allies against the plains tribes. The tribes made use of the plentiful natural resources of the Northern Rocky Mountains and were prosperous and self-supporting.

The United States federal government's encroachment on Flathead Indian Reservation affairs originated with the 1855 Hellgate treaty. In the treaty, the tribes relinquished their claim to most of western Montana but "reserved from the lands above ceded" the Flathead Indian Reservation. The government promised that the reservation "shall be set apart, and, so far as necessary, surveyed and marked out for the exclusive use and benefit of said confederated tribes as an Indian reservation."[1]

The fifty years after the treaty was signed witnessed explosive growth in the white population in Montana and the decimation of the big game population—especially the buffalo. During the same time, white settlers established farms on fertile land that had previously provided wild plant food for the tribal commissary. The Flathead Reservation tribes faced a crisis with the loss of the resources on which the traditional tribal economy was based. Unlike the plains tribes that fell back on government rations with the loss of the buffalo and other resources, the Flathead Reservation tribes developed an economy by 1905 based on herds of horses and cattle on the open range and farms raising grain and household vegetables. Rations were only issued to the old and infirm and in exchange for work done for the agency. The government never controlled the food supply of the Flathead Reservation tribes which greatly enhanced their independence. Flathead Agent Peter Ronan emphasized the tribes' economic self-sufficiency in his 1886 annual report which included the following table:

| Articles | Estimated Pounds. | Allowance for one year for each Indian. Pounds. |
|---|---|---|
| Bacon | 12,500 | $6^{1}/_{4}$ |
| Beans | 1,600 | $^{4}/_{5}$ |
| Coffee | 3,500 | $1^{3}/_{4}$ |
| Flour | 25,000 | $12^{1}/_{2}$ |
| Rice | 1,300 | $^{13}/_{20}$ |
| Oatmeal | 700 | $^{7}/_{20}$ |
| Sugar | 9,500 | $4^{3}/_{4}$ |
| Tea | 700 | $^{7}/_{20}$ |
| Salt | 1,400 | $^{7}/_{10}^{2}$ |

The parsimonious government rations supplied through the Flathead Agency insured that most tribal members were self-supporting during the second half of the nineteenth century. The people were able to expand their stock raising and farming to take up the slack from the loss of traditional resources.

By 1905, before the allotment policy was forced on the tribes, the historical evidence suggests that the Flathead Reservation tribes were not only self-supporting but relatively well off. On September 20, 1903, Indian Inspector Arthur M. Tinker described the economic progress made by the reservation tribes:

> The Indians and mixed-bloods (of the latter class there are many) of this reservation are said to be generally industrious and seem to be quite progressive. From all indications they appear to be in good financial condition. No supplies or rations are issued except to a few aged and infirm. It cannot be said that they are easily governed, as a large number of them do not want to obey their agent in any particular. They do their business in their own way and never consult him unless they get into trouble: most

of them drink intoxicating liquor to excess. Agent [W. H.] Smead has caused several whiskey dealers to be arrested, tried, convicted and punished for selling liquor to Indians, still they seem to have no trouble in getting all the liquor they have money to pay for. Most of the males wear citizen clothes and wear a blanket in addition during cold weather. Some few of the full-bloods and most of the mixed-bloods speak some English.

Nearly all of the females speak nothing but their native language and wear their native dress, there are, however, some few exceptions to the general rule.

A large majority of them are good farmers for Indians and cultivate quite good sized farms, which usually produce good crops. It is estimated that more than 17,000 acres of land are now under cultivation, the work being done by Indian labor. The crop produced consists principally of wheat, oats, potatoes and vegetables; they also cut a large amount of hay which they feed to their cattle, the surplus which they bale and ship it, is estimated this year will be about 1,000 tons they sell to the whiteman off the reservation.

They find ready sale for all the surplus products they produce at good prices. As this has been a favorable season, it is expected that the crop to be harvested will be large.

Each year the number of acres of land cultivated has increased.

Several of the mixed-bloods and... [white men married to Indian women] have fenced large tracts of land they claim as their own.

All the Indians have fairly good houses: many of the mixed-bloods have very good houses and outbuildings which compare favorably with those owned by the better class of white farmers living off the reservation.

I am informed that members of the different tribes of this reservation, own from 25,000 to 30,000 head of cattle and the Father's [sic] at St. Ignatius Mission own about 4,000 head; They also own quite a number of horses.

The Indians usually take good care of their cattle; they herd them on the ranges during the grazing season and cut hay to feed them in the winter; they sell them at any time, to any person they desire and never consult their agent; this has been the prevailing custom here for many years....[3]

Unfortunately, the early twentieth century imposition of the allotment policy on the Flathead Reservation undermined the pre-1905 progress and left tribal members in poverty. Allotment resulted in the forced sale of "surplus" land on the reservation for less than its full value. According to the U.S. Court of Claims, the value of the land sold under the allotment act was $7,410,000, and the tribe only received $1,783,549 or 24 cents on the dollar.[4] When the tribes were forced to sell their land for less than market value, their future income was reduced. Montana Congressman Joseph M. Dixon was able to use a recent U.S. Supreme Court decision to get Congress to impose the policy on the Flathead Reservation without tribal consent.[5] The bill provided that the "surplus" lands were to be "disposed of under the general provisions of the homestead, mineral, and town-site laws of the United States," which meant that white homesteaders got the reservation land for the discounted prices that the government charged for sale of publicly owned land.[6]

Research by Harvard trained economist, Ronald Trosper, indicated that the allotment of the reservation accounted for virtually all of the differences between the 1969 average per capita income of tribal members and the average per capita income for all United States residents that year. This would suggest that poverty on the Flathead Reservation in the late twentieth century was largely the consequence of the forced sale or theft of tribal assets through allotment.[7] The lack of tribal consent and the perception that the tribes were being mistreated provided the painful backdrop for the tribal complaints and actions described in Voggesser's study.

To complicate matters further, the 1908 act setting up the Flathead Irrigation Project stipulated that the government appropriations for project construction were reimbursable. The money from tribal land sales and other assets was to be used to reimburse the federal treasury for the appropriations to build the irrigation project. The tribes would then be paid back from the money the white homesteaders paid for their land.[8] In other words, the tribes were liable for building an irrigation project that mostly served white homesteaders. This policy was not reversed until 1916 when the irrigation construction charges were made a lien on the land owned by white and Indian water users.[9]

Almost from the beginning, the white settlers claimed that they could not afford to pay for the construction and operation of the irrigation project. They repeatedly insisted that the money invested in the project did not increase their agricultural income enough to pay the cost of the project. This was despite the generous subsidy forced on the tribes who were not paid for the land and water rights used by the project. Fortunately, the irrigation project developed a business selling electricity on the reservation, which was making a profit. In the end, under a compromise reached in 1948, the power users on the reservation repaid the federal treasury for most of the construction loans.[10]

A final point of context for Voggesser's study is that, despite decades of on and off construction, the Flathead Irrigation Project was never completed. In 1962, the Bureau of Indian Affairs drew up a plan for completion of the project which would expand its capacity to catch spring runoff water for irrigation use in the summer, but it was never fully implemented. The plan called for a small expansion of the number of acres irrigated, lining of canals to reduce seepage losses, and construction of a major new water storage facility in the Jocko Valley.[11]

**********

Chapter 1 of Voggesser's study, "Making the Flathead Reservation 'Blossom as the Rose,'" traces the history of irrigation on the Flathead Reservation from the late nineteenth century to the John Collier administration in the 1930s. The Flathead Irrigation Project was authorized by a 1908 federal law written by then-Senator Joseph Dixon. The development of the irrigation system was handicapped by on-again and off-again congressional appropriations and bureaucratic conflict between the U.S. Bureau of Reclamation, which supervised the construction and operation of the project, and the U.S. Bureau of Indian Affairs, which actually received the appropriated funds. Dixon's plan to pay for the project with tribal funds further complicated and aggravated the situation. As mentioned above, in 1916 Congress passed a law making the Indian and white land owners liable for the irrigation costs and returning the tribal funds to the tribes. As the "surplus" lands and allotments were sold to white men, the project had continual problems reconciling the conflicting claims of the government, which expected reimbursement for construction charges; the tribes; and the white settlers. The conflict over the Flathead Irrigation Project spilled into the debate about timber harvest on the reservation and the development of the hydropower site at the foot of Flathead Lake.

Chapter 2, "A Lot of Trouble About Wood," surveys the early history of lumbering on the Flathead Reservation. In the twentieth century, the government was in a rush to sell as much reservation timber as possible so the proceeds could be used to reimburse the federal treasury for the irrigation construction costs. At the same time, however, the government was developing a national policy of resource conservation and sustained yield forestry. To complicate matters even further, the 1904 Flathead Allotment Act provided for timberlands on the reservation to be handled differently from the regular agricultural homesteads. White squatters and the government haggled over the disposal of timberlands for decades. High volumes of timber were harvested on the reservation during the 1910s and 1920s, but the national depression destroyed the market for reservation timber during the 1930s.

The final chapter, "The 'Indian Muscle Shoals,'" traces the battle over the ownership and development of the hydropower site at the foot of Flathead Lake during the 1920s and 1930s. Since the Flathead Irrigation Project had invested some funds in a tunnel to use the hydropower site to pump irrigation water, the dam site became entangled in the controversy over paying the irrigation construction costs. As a private citizen, John Collier headed the American Indian Defense Association which supported the efforts of the Flathead Reservation tribes to keep control of the dam site. During the late 1920s, the battle over ownership and licensing of the site assumed national dimensions. Voggesser provides an exciting summary of the struggles. The Confederated Salish and Kootenai Tribes wanted Walter H. Wheeler to get the license, but the Federal Power Commission decided to give the development license to the Montana Power Company instead. The license for the dam and compensation for the tribes continued to be a battleground for the rest of the twentieth and start of the twenty-first centuries.

By the time of the publication of this book in 2017, the Confederated Salish and Kootenai Tribes has taken over ownership of the hydropower dam at the foot of Flathead Lake and the management of the Flathead Irrigation Project. Hopefully, Voggesser's study will help reservation residents—Indian and white—better understand the years of struggle that made it possible for the tribes to get where they are today.

# Chapter 1

# Making the Flathead Reservation "Blossom as the Rose"

# The Flathead Irrigation Project

In 1929, Frederick Newell, former Director of the Reclamation Service, looked back at thirty years of federal management of Indian natural resources. He mused that in 1900, "The enthusiasm of youth was aroused by the vision of the great resources…little known to the public. If wisely handled they spelled prosperity to the Indians. No one seemed to be giving thought to the problems of protection of the [Indian's] property, nor of the water rights." Eventually, the Reclamation Service and the Indian Office worked together to develop Indian irrigation, the former building the projects and the latter handling financing and Indian "education." The "ultimate object" of managing and utilizing natural resources was "the improvement of the condition of the Indian in self-support and in the qualities which [would] make him a good citizen." No shortage of idealism and ambition existed among those involved in creating federal policy on tribal water. The questions, Newell surmised, were whether the ideals of conservation had been realized, what were the "lessons taught," and how had the government applied those lessons "to attain the best results for the Indians and for the common welfare"? The greatest obstacle had been to agree upon the end to be attained. Indian irrigation was as much a moral as an economic project.[1]

To understand the dilemma over irrigation it is imperative to recognize both how white settlement and Indian allotment worked out on the Flathead Reservation, and larger patterns of migration and land acquisition in Montana and the West. Montana belied the Turnerian belief that the frontier was a nineteenth-century phenomenon. Montana was the last "frontier," the last that exhibited the quintessential ethic of nineteenth-century American individualism. The state represented one of the few regions after 1900 to offer arable land for newcomers. Between 1900 and 1920, 200,000 people flooded into Montana, nearly doubling the population. The Enlarged Homestead Act of 1909 and the Stock Raising Homestead Act of 1916 pulled in immigrants from the Midwest and other regions, opening the way for the settlement of more lands than were claimed under the Homestead Act in the entire nineteenth century.[2] The new settlers, or "honyockers," that flooded into Montana from 1900 to 1920 took up more than forty percent of the entire land area of Montana. These people were the "Joads," as one historian of Montana put it, before the nation ever reached the Great Depression. They arrived with hope, courage, and dreams of great wealth on the high end, and, at the least, comfort and security. Their ambitions carried them into the conflict over land and irrigated agriculture on the Flathead Reservation.[3]

*Irrigation In the Nineteenth Century*

The concentration on federally managed Indian irrigation projects in the twentieth century ignored more than a half-century of work undertaken by Indians and other industrious individuals. When Jesuit missionaries arrived in the Flathead territory in the early 1840s, they helped Indians develop irrigation to water fruit trees and provide "moral and agricultural education." By the 1880s, the promise of irrigation caused one Indian Office

Chief Charlo, ca. 1910 (NA 8NS-75-97-221, box 7, 222)

administrator to conclude that with fuller development of reservation natural resources the "Indians would be rich." Water would produce organized agriculture and more orderly Indians. Flathead Indian Agent Peter Ronan attempted to lure Chief Charlo's band away from the Bitterroot Valley and onto the reservation with promises of irrigation. Ronan's "good scheme" for constructing ditches would provide employment, promote agriculture and settlement, and, he hoped, make the reservation "blossom as the rose." Individual Indians simply did not have the "capital or ability" to construct the projects. What Ronan envisioned was the beginning of a much larger federal program for the recreation of the Indian environment.[4]

In one sense, the irrigation of Indian lands was a part of the larger push for developing the U.S. West at the end of the nineteenth century. In 1886, the Secretary of the Interior concluded that making the "immense areas of fertile land" in the West inhabitable required an irrigation enterprise backed by "accumulated capital" and under a "single management"—the federal government was the best candidate for that job. Nevertheless, irrigating Indian lands posed greater difficulties than providing water for non-Indian farmers. The federal government would not only have to provide the capital and expertise to construct the projects, but, more significantly in federal officials' eyes, make Indians into good, yeoman farmers. Otherwise, all the water in the West would not put Indians on the path to self-support.[5]

The well-intentioned goal of making Indians into irrigation farmers also came with less benign and less admirable beliefs. Many federal officials judged Indians in terms of Anglo culture. Not surprisingly, Indian Office personnel viewed Indians as "repugnant" to manual labor, as "very poor material out of which to make farmers," and as lacking the "foresight, good husbandry, economy, and persistence necessary to make farming successful." Furthermore, Indians were "easily discouraged," the failure of one crop "almost fatal to their hopes," and making them "inclined to give up further effort." The Commissioner of Indian Affairs surmised, "It cannot be expected that under such circumstances all or even many will...step from the position of ignorant, shiftless, lazy savages to that of successful independent farmers." However, that was just what the Bureau of Indian Affairs (BIA) intended to do. Irrigation was the linchpin to making that project successful.[6]

The 1890s can be seen as a turning point on the Flathead Reservation. Agent Peter Ronan's early efforts at building canals paid off. The Indian Office authorized Ronan to expend $5,000 to construct a six-mile ditch. Diverting water from the Jocko River to agricultural land had "proven a success beyond all expectation." Irrigated crops were abundant, while crops without water failed. However, the ditch proved too small to meet the full needs of the tribe. Thus, in what would be a consistent plea from reservation agents and field inspectors for the next eighteen years, one official requested larger and more frequent appropriations. Without that commitment to irrigation, there would be no "assurance whatever" of growing ample crops from the "waste lands" and arid soil, or of reaping "thrifty" and diligent Indian farmers from their customs of "idleness and dependency."[7]

While Indian Office officials urged greater dedication to funding the irrigation of tribal lands, the Secretary of the Interior exhorted congress to enact comprehensive laws to determine the "national policy in this business." The U.S. Geological Survey undertook a vast project for surveying the public lands of the West to identify reservoir sites for development to benefit settlers. White settlement across the West and the resulting reduction of reservations meant the "confining of Indians to ever-narrowing borders," and made the "problem of their support one of increasing difficulty and urgency." The Commissioner of Indian Affairs argued, "White people are able to combine in the creation of expensive and extensive irrigating plans, which the Indians can not do…. The matter can not be safely deferred any longer."[8]

Comparing crops irrigated by the Jocko River ditch with unwatered sections of the Flathead Reservation certainly taught "an object lesson on the value of irrigation." Inspectors urged the BIA to supplement the existing project on the west side of the Jocko with additional canals on the east side of the river, believing that would make the Indians self-supporting. The disastrous drought that struck the plains in the early 1890s reinforced the need for water. In 1892, the BIA authorized the first substantial amount of $58,000 for irrigation construction on Indian reservations. The amount appropriated was meager in comparison with the vast expanse of tribal lands. Still, while some Flatheads "adhere[d] to the traditional blanket," a good number took up construction work and agriculture pursuits with a new vigor in the early 1890s.[9]

Agent Ronan's promise of irrigated land lured Charlo's band from the Bitterroot to the Jocko Valley. A couple of years later, in 1893, Ronan complained that they remained a "trifling class of Indians," but argued that the newly irrigated tracts left them with no excuse for not fencing and cultivating their land. Ronan was emblematic of the men in his line of work. He certainly had the interests of the Indians in mind when developing the irrigation system. Yet, like many in the Indian Office, he quickly shifted his comments from praise to derision. In fact, he is a good example of the convenient forgetfulness on the part of BIA employees. Ronan argued that the Indians, without reason, were "lazy" and slow to construct farms. However, Charlo's band refused to fence and cultivate their land because they were promised that if they relocated, the government would provide all the components of established farms for them. The Indians took literally the government's treaty promises to take care of them "for all time." Still, when Agent Joseph Carter replaced Ronan in 1893, he complimented the irrigation enterprise as "a most important factor in advancing habits of industry" and self-support. A few of the "most enterprising mixed-bloods" had planted gardens and orchards, and the "encouraging effect" of irrigation had promoted the construction of permanent homes.[10]

In the mid-1890s, BIA inspectors and Agent Carter significantly increased proposals for enlarged irrigation works. One inspector suggested a series of canals and ditches fifty-five miles in length at a cost of $61,000—more than the entire budget for irrigating all Indian lands ever proposed in a single year.[11] The "civilizing and encouraging results" of irrigation in the Jocko Valley led many Indians to demand further development at no cost to the tribe. This was not an unworthy request, but the logical result of a string of promises made by the Indian Office. Despite its pledges and promotion, the BIA failed to take action. Though the "civilization" and "advancement" of the tribe depended on irrigation, little was done to improve and add to the canals, except the work done by the Indians themselves. One field inspector concluded in the fall of 1896, "It is a deplorable fact that the exceeding drought of this season has caused a failure of crops, excepting in favored localities where there was an opportunity to irrigate, and where advantage was taken of the water supply."[12]

The shortcomings of federal management of tribal irrigation did not go unnoticed. Officials candidly admitted that the government had treated with the Flathead and broken the promises for irrigated farms and that the Indians "would be kept as long as they lived by the Government." These frank admissions had little bearing on Indian Office action. What the complications of Indian irrigation on the Flathead Reservation did cause, however, was increasing pleas for better organization, more funding, and a more honest analysis of Indian affairs. The BIA had focused too narrowly on agriculture, neglecting that more Flathead Indians made a living from livestock than crops, Inspector W. J. McConnell warned. "[I]f by any action of ours we make it impossible for them to succeed in that enterprise, we do them a great wrong." By seeing agriculture as the only road to civilization and advancement, BIA administrators failed to envision other possibilities for Indian "self-support." This early clarification of the problems of Indian administration highlighted what would become a consistent dilemma in the twentieth century.[13]

Several other issues confounded irrigation. Agency inspectors increasingly argued that it was a mistake for each new reservation agent—

often with little experience—to map out his own course for irrigation work. Instead, the complexities of the work required a "a man skilled in the construction of ditches" to draw up the plans, and that the agent be required to follow them in the way the Indian Office directed. Increasingly by the late-1890s, non-Indians—looking forward to the allotment reservations and sale of surplus land—began squatting on Indian lands before the BIA appraised them. These "trespassers" began claiming water rights on the land regardless of ownership and tribal rights. Second only to the Indian Office's lack of an adequate engineering staff to prepare coherent plans, funding was the most essential problem. The BIA considered having the Flathead cede a part of their lands to finance construction. Meanwhile, the appropriations for Indian irrigation remained paltry, with as little as $3,000 a year going to Flathead. Reservation officials were beginning to realize that they had "nearly reached the limit in this work for individual effort and enterprise." The Indian Office proved reluctant to commit to larger works, falsely hoping that the Indians could get by on "small and comparatively cheap ones."[14]

Despite the limitations of irrigation on Flathead, and if BIA statistics can be trusted, the Indians managed decent progress by the turn of the century. Between 1890 and 1900, the area cultivated by Indians increased from 900 to 11,000 acres, and the production of wheat and oats increased from about 10,000 bushels for each crop to 41,000 bushels of wheat and nearly 35,000 bushels of oats. The production of vegetables rose comparably. Much of the increased yield came from irrigated land. The "land accessible to the streams on which water [could] be turned with little labor and expense" had been claimed, and it became increasingly "difficult for young men to find suitable lands to undertake to cultivate." In fact, Indian Agent W. H. Smead complained that lands that would produce crops without irrigation and those on which water could be easily and cheaply carried "are in possession of white men and mixed bloods principally, many of whom have no rights on the reservation, and many others whose rights are much in doubt."[15]

Besides the monopolization of large tracts by a few individuals, the lack of available, irrigable land stemmed from the government's failure to provide water to hundreds of thousands of acres of valuable, fertile land. The situation meant many Indians had no land to farm. It also meant that the Flathead were left in "idleness" and that they had become "demoralized and [were] a menace to the welfare of others." Irrigation was not only key to employment and self-support, but a solution to "immoral" or improper behavior. The increasing fervor of complaints indicated that allotment and irrigation would go hand in hand.[16]

*The Vision For A New West, A Vision For A New Indian*

While the 1890s stood as a turning point in the mere recognition that irrigation offered a possible solution to the "Indian Problem," it was in the twentieth century that constructing vast irrigation projects on tribal lands became the single most viable—and most ennobled—answer to making Indians into responsible citizens. Federal irrigation, like federal Indian administration, was a program founded on the unstable bedrock of idealism. The new century brought both new ambitions for the West and a vision for a new Indian.

If any one figure symbolized these aspirations, that figure would be Frederick H. Newell. Later the Director of the Reclamation Service and a keynote figure in the conservation movement, Newell made his initial impact on Indian irrigation as a hydrographer for the U.S. Geological Survey. In a report to the Board of Indian Commissioners, Newell highlighted the failures of past irrigation work and a plan for the future. Though Newell did not exactly fall in line with the board's conservative belief that the only route for Indians lay in complete assimilation into white culture, that creed, nonetheless, contributed to irrigation plans on Indian reservations. Newell contended that the government had crowded Indians onto the most arid and least accessible lands. The government spent hundreds of thousands of dollars on educating Indians—"in trying to make them into farmers or stock

Alex Matt and view of irrigation canal built by him about 1890. Photo ca. Sept. 1910.
(NA 8NS-75-97-221, box 1, F15)

raisers"—but had not supplied the key "element of success, the necessary water supply." Out of all the money spent on Indian irrigation, probably only twenty-five percent of the investment had been of use. Newell criticized, "On nearly all sides are evidences of hasty and costly work and imperfect results."

If the money spent on irrigated agriculture for Indians had been "wasted," then Newell had some answers. Part of the blame could be put on the bureaucracy of a "too highly organized administration," but the bulk of the problem lay in the imperfect "system" of allotment. The government settled the Indians on small tracts of land along streams with small ditches. Then, it opened the remainder of the reservation to settlement, with the result that "the white man, using his better judgment, has taken out a larger canal heading above the Indians." For the Indian "to make progress as a farmer," the government needed to protect Indian water rights, as well as provided them tracts of land sufficient for cultivation. Newell made even more troublesome observations, and ones which would come back to haunt the Indian Office in the future. He concluded, "The more rules and regulations, especially those laid down upon theoretical lines, the more easy it is to waste and fritter away opportunities and to accomplish nothing." The federal agencies which would be most "efficient and economical" would be "those having the fewest regulations and in which the responsible chiefs do not hesitate to break an office rule." Utilizing irrigation to solve the "Indian problem" required pluck and vigor, not conservatism.[17]

Indian Office tenets were based on conviction, but rarely on decisiveness. It would take another four years, until 1904, for action to be taken on the allotment of the Flathead Reservation, and an additional four to commit to irrigation. However, the two undertakings were intimately connected. The long-standing complaints about the lack of suitable water supply coupled with frequent crop losses to drought helped make the case for the irrigation project. Yet other intentions lay behind the scheme. Reclaiming the land certainly offered solutions to drought, "idleness," and making agricultural Indians, but irrigation also promised to render the reservation more valuable for white settlement. Allotment of the Flathead Reservation coincided with a changed emphasis on irrigation, and with results Newell would both have expected and could never have possibly foreseen.[18]

*Formulating the Indian Irrigation Projects*

In the early twentieth century, demands from the arid West significantly altered the Indian Office's attitude toward irrigation on tribal lands. The Reclamation Act of 1902 set the tone for water development. The BIA began to organize a more efficient force of employees and conduct surveys for irrigating reservations. Since the 1880s, it had intended irrigation as a financial venture for eliminating poverty, hunger, and disdain for agriculture as well as a mission of moralization and civilization; the Reclamation Act provided stronger impetus. The western, non-Indian clamor for irrigation made Indian water rights a vital concern. In fact, the attention focused on irrigation made protection of all tribal natural resources paramount. In 1907, to ensure effective and organized progress, the Reclamation and Indian Bureaus formed an alliance for the construction of the Indian Irrigation Projects. The systems would guarantee beneficial use regardless of Indian inclinations.[19]

Grand schemes by the federal government have never been in short supply, but the Indian Irrigation Projects certainly proved daunting. The most fundamental obstacle was funding. In 1907, Congress allotted $3,000 for the Reclamation Service to begin reconnaissance work on the Flathead Reservation, and a year later appropriated $50,000 for comprehensive surveys preliminary to construction. Yet, funding the actual construction of the Flathead Irrigation Project attested to the difficulty of such a large enterprise. Financing reclamation first relied on allotment, and then on the sale of surplus property to non-Indians. However, Flathead was unique among the Indian Irrigation Projects. The subsidization of the project also relied on proceeds from the sale of tribal timber. Allotting tracts to Indians and selling the surplus property proved complicated enough without throwing in the complexity of timber sales. Classifying and selling the merchantable timber for the "great irrigation enterprise" delayed construction for several years.[20]

Meanwhile, more serious problems arose to challenge the irrigation plans. In the rush to allot lands, the BIA failed to properly coordinate with the Reclamation Service. In the fall of 1909, Indians protested the construction of a number of reservoirs because they had been allotted land within those sites. The Reclamation Service dismissed the complaints as trivial, arguing that the Flathead had made few improvements on the land and thus other allotments could easily be substituted. The Indians would not be so easily disregarded; by November, the Flathead had hired an attorney. Through their counsel, the Indians contended that John Sloan, the allotting agent, "by threats and duress," forced them to relinquish their allotments in the reservoir sites. The BIA attempted to absolve itself of responsibility by claiming that Sloan acted against its wishes. In turn, the Reclamation Service claimed it had no knowledge of the case, except "a casual remark" by the supervising engineer that Sloan "seemed to be active and efficient."[21]

Despite claims of innocence, the dispute suggested significant shortcomings. First, it indicated the lack of coordination between the Indian

Louie Pierre at work on his allotment, successful Indian farmer, July 1914.
(NA 8NS-75-97-221, box 7, F256)

and Reclamation Bureaus; having a cooperative agreement did not promise proper communication. Next, agents in the field often misinterpreted orders that came from higher up in the ranks. Presumably, the BIA directed Sloan to gain "voluntary" relinquishments of the reservoir site allotments, while actually completing that task required Sloan to use "threats" and other "undue methods." Furthermore, the ideals, or goals, of the Indian Office and the Reclamation Service did not always mesh. Each bureau attempted to shift blame to the other.

Frederick H. Abbott, Acting Commissioner of Indian Affairs, lodged the veiled threat that if the Reclamation Service's work on reservoir sites involved forced removal of Indians "it might embarrass that Bureau considerably," particularly if it had to give the land back to the Indians. However, "as a matter of justice," it might have to be done. A. P. Davis, Acting Director of the Reclamation Service, replied that the reservoirs were necessary "to the highest use of the waters of the Reservation, and if they cannot be obtained, the water must perpetually run to waste." The Reclamation Service intended no injustice to the Indians, he continued, but some means had to be found "by which individual interests should not be allowed to stand permanently in the way of a larger development." The principal of legal condemnation and withdrawal of lands was implicit in the Reclamation Act, and on Indian reservations, could "be invoked to legally dispossess unwilling claimants in reservoir sites necessary for the development of the Reservation."[22]

The confusion over allotment and irrigation was not that simple. In theory, the BIA's argument revealed its unwillingness to breach the rights of individual Indians even if it meant neglecting the supposed good of the whole tribe. Conversely, the Reclamation Service was guilty of being more focused on the "large development" than the desires of the Indians themselves. However, both bureaus stumbled over their explanations. H. N. Savage, supervising engineer of the Indian Projects for the Reclamation Service, contended that his bureau placed primary emphasis on the "actual necessary requirements" of the allottees; it followed that irrigation development was "a necessity to the allottees to enable them to get a living from the allotments." Savage insinuated that living up to the Indian Office's stated goal of making Indians into farmers required irrigation works, as well as accepting the repercussions of canceling a few allotments. In short, the greater end to be attained through the Flathead Irrigation Project and the rights of every Indian were not always mutually compatible. The initial bickering between the two bureaus on land and water were minor compared to what lay ahead.[23]

### An "Indian Project" Or A "White Project"?

Though neither the Indian Office nor the Reclamation Service recognized it early on, from the beginning the Flathead Irrigation Project blurred the line between being an Indian or a white persons' project. It is easy to blame either bureau, and both were certainly at fault. However, the problems also stemmed from the desires of white settlers versus Indian inhabitants, profit motives pitted against cultural values, and the contradicting goals and policies of the Indian and Reclamation Bureaus.

In late 1909, the Reclamation Service began construction of the Flathead Project, and in 1910 the government opened the reservation to white settlement. The work needed to be pushed as fast as possible because whites had already taken up a large portion of reservation lands and these people were "clamoring for water." Not enough water existed for everyone, and if the Reclamation Service did not finish the ditches to supply irrigation to Indian lands "the speculative element among the whites [would] dispute the claim of the Indians to the water and deprive them of it." Homesteading on the reservation also posed serious problems. Many who took up land prior to the opening of the reservation had squatted on unclassified lands. To establish the proper value of the property the BIA needed to designate each tract according to its resources as either grazing, agricultural, timbered, or a mixture of those characteristics. Until the Indian Office classified the lands, settlers gained no rights by settlement. In the fervor to take up property and construct improvements, many homesteaders failed to realize that without classification a good possibility existed that they would lose everything.[24]

The complications of settlement arose from a complex mix of misunderstandings and misrepresentations. A BIA commission originally appraised and classified the lands of the reservation under the 1904 law. However, allotment and irrigation drastically altered the value and classification of a large part of the reservation. Most Indians received their allotments before the Reclamation Service made surveys for irrigation. Once completed, the plans for reservoir sites, ditches, and canals required the cancellation of Indian allotments in locations that conflicted with the project and their exchange for different tracts.

Providing land for Indians not only delayed settlement by non-Indians, but ran directly against Anglo-American ideas of progress. Many homesteaders—or squatters—saw the delays as a conspiracy against whites and characteristic of "pin-headed policies" that flew in the face of development. Some argued that the Indian Office "retarded" development by halting all leasing of Indian lands to white farmers. This was done to encourage Indians to farm their own tracts. Congress had opened the Flathead Reservation for settlement and "improvement." Now, homesteaders claimed, "some big bureau chief at Washington" favored the "blanket Indian" in a way that proved detrimental to the tribe, the agricultural growth of the region, and to the profit of the progressive mixed-blood Indians and whites alike.[25]

Still, with prospects of good agricultural land and cheap irrigation, the non-Indian population burgeoned. The reservation's newspaper, *The Ronan Pioneer*, was the voice of these people. Its editors put a spin on local issues, fanning the flames of conflict and speculation. They claimed they had "no purely selfish motives," but asked "only fairness for the white man in the same ratio as with the wards of the government." Government officials saw the situation differently. "There is a tendency to criticize the department," Flathead Superintendent Fred C. Morgan remarked. "It is charged in some quarters that the endeavor is to retard the development of the reserve. This is not so." The delays in irrigation construction and land settlement represented the typical "routine [of] departmental matters," and no more delay—or "conspiracy"—existed in this case than in any other government endeavor.[26]

Morgan fought an uphill battle by defending government policy. The *Pioneer* proclaimed itself the guardian of the Flathead Reservation community, Indians and whites alike. By pushing Indians into agriculture, rather than allowing them to lease, the editors argued that the government left the tribe "rich in lands," but poor in prospects. The paper cited the case of widowed Indian Mary Howlett and her children. She had received an allotment of 680 acres, but unable to farm it, eked out a living by selling a few eggs and some butter from three cows. "It is a shame," the *Pioneer* declared, "that people with land rich in soil like these unfortunates have, should be allowed to freeze and starve when so many are seeking the privilege of working the land and would willingly pay a good rental for the chance." Meanwhile, local commercial clubs assailed the Interior Department with reports of the "crying need" of settlers and the "necessity of hastening the completion" of the irrigation work to prevent "general suffering."[27]

In what would be a recurrent theme—the lack of funding—remained a key obstacle to constructing the irrigation project to the satisfaction of all parties involved. Financing increasingly focused on two questions: how would the government handle the appropriations, and who would be required to reimburse the government for its costs? The initial outlay came from congressional appropriations to the BIA, which, in turn, would be reimbursed by the sale of surplus Indian land and timber. However, as the system increasingly came to involve whites who purchased Indian land, questions arose as to whether Indians should pay for water going to non-Indians. Next, should the Flathead and whites alike pay for both construction as well as operation and maintenance charges once the irrigation system was up and running? Moreover, if an allottee sold his land to a white man, should the purchaser pay the full construction charges and operation and maintenance costs, or simply the value of the land plus operation and maintenance? While homesteads had the same obligation as individually-owned Indian lands, purchased allotments made a problematic situation more difficult. The situation proved detrimental to the Flathead. For an allottee to get the full value of his land, he had to wait until the government completed the project—an uncertain prospect at best. Consequently, an Indian in dire need of income would have to sell short to survive.[28]

Back of these problems lay a unique sense of entitlement on the part of non-Indians, or as the *Pioneer* put it, "give the farmer fair play and do it now." Americans have frequently confused "right" with "privilege," but in the context of the Flathead Irrigation Project the misconception became much more disruptive. "The average man is somewhat surprised," the *Pioneer* exclaimed, that the government expected homesteaders to pay for water. The white farmer paid the "Indian price" for land, paid government fees and commissions, and expended "his every dollar to establish a home for himself and family," and now the government asked him to pay for irrigation. The paper's editors thought it hypocrisy for congress to pass river and harbor bills to defray the cost of development in the East, and not do the same for settlers in the West. After all, the agricultural products of western farms contributed an equal value to the nation as the imports that passed through eastern ports. The "talk of what the government is doing for the arid west is all bosh," the paper declared, "the farmers are doing it for themselves."[29]

Homesteaders' complaints stemmed from decisions made by the Indian and Reclamation Bureaus. The BIA was simply unwilling to front money for an enterprise that promised no certainty of reimbursement. Congress made reimbursable appropriations for Indian irrigation construction to the BIA. Then the Reclamation Service paid for the costs of constructing the Indian Projects and the BIA reimbursed the Reclamation Service, but the Service objected to this practice when it had obligations to use its appropriations to pay for non-Indian irrigation projects. This hesitancy to expend funds was unique for a government agency. After all, the Reclamation Service supplied funds for its other irrigation projects, counting on farmers to pay it back in the future. To stay out of debt, the BIA decided that tribal funds must cover past and current rather than future work. In the initial years of the project, and until money from tribal timber and land sales began to accrue in sufficient amounts, the project would proceed at a sluggish pace. The cautiousness also reflected concerns about Indians' attitudes. Many Flathead protested against the use of their money to build the reclamation ditches, instead requesting that tribal income be distributed in per capita payments to cover individual expenses and purchase livestock and equipment. Despite the *Pioneer's* claims to the contrary, the tribe had a reasonable fear that the "white man want[ed] it all on the reservation," not just the water.[30]

By 1912, white residents concluded that the "proper development of the country" required them to take matters into their own hands, and *The Ronan Pioneer* led the charge. The primary task focused on the purchase and settlement of surplus tribal property. In this endeavor, other natural resources besides water began to play a primary role. "The scheme," the editors proclaimed, "is to have the government appraise the land at a price which will make it profitable for anyone to homestead the land and let the timber go with the land.... There is no telling what the country would develop into...should this timbered land be placed on the market." The *Pioneer* and its readers wanted to put the land to agricultural use; timber was secondary. By replacing trees with consumable crops, the value of adjacent areas would increase. What this great "scheme" required, the *Pioneer* declared, was "the education of the department at Washington along proper lines," and they intended to teach officials that the interest of settlers, rather than Indians, would not only benefit Flathead's white population, but the nation.[31]

Pierre Joseph on mower on field of Louie Pierre July 1914.
Pierre Joseph was employed by Louie Pierre.
(NA 8NS-75-97-221, box 7, F259)

Louie Pierre and haystack, July 1914.
(NA 8NS-75-97-221, box 7, F259)

This attempt to "educate" the Washington office of the peoples' best interests produced a conflict between settlement and development and the management of natural resources. Flathead's white population believed easterners saw western homesteaders as "land thiefs," getting something for nothing. The *Pioneer* retorted, "While the eastern conservationist is pointing his finger at the homesteader and crying thief, it would not be out of place to ask how matters are conducted in their own pet departments—having to do with conservation, forestry, power, reclamation and the allied grafts, wherein thousands of incompetents wax fat yearly at the public crib." Three months after the *Pioneer* put forth its "great scheme" the General Land Office confronted the results. Squatters flooded onto tracts classified as timber lands, hoping to reap the easy profit promised by the *Pioneer*. While the government lobbed allegations at speculators and squatters, the *Pioneer* struck back with accusations of a Land Office conspiracy against innocent settlers. Both parties ignored a key issue: everyone intended to get rid of the trees—no matter their value—on the assumption that irrigated agriculture was worth more and did more to boost the price of land.[32]

The dispute between white settlers and the government reached the higher echelons of the Interior Department. In 1913, Reclamation Service Director Frederick H. Newell acknowledged the plight of Indian and non-Indian residents of the Indian Irrigation Projects. The sluggish pace of construction and delays in appropriations threatened both the survival of project residents, and the integrity of the Reclamation Service. Against Newell's objections, congress reduced the expenditures for irrigation on the Fort Peck Reservation in favor of larger appropriations "for the benefit of whites on the Flathead Reservation." Interior Secretary Franklin K. Lane also recommended a delay in collecting construction charges from white settlers. The decision highlighted a key tenet of the Reclamation Service: a firm belief in the viability of the family farm in the West, and the dedication and diligence of the common man. Lane wanted reclamation projects, and thus irrigation farmers, to be successful. However, the move reflected a consistent delusion on the part of the government. Farmers did not want more time to pay for water, but for the government to waive the debt entirely. The idealistic faith in the independent, yeoman farmer did not match with what the farmer felt the government owed him.[33]

Despite his empathy for settlers, even Secretary Lane admitted that Flathead was first and foremost an Indian Project. Whites complained that they came to Flathead "at the invitation of the government," relying upon its promises that they would be treated fairly. Lane's "lip service" was simply the admission that irrigation development would provide water to Indians first and whites second. Lane's disclosure reflected not only the slow progress on irrigation work, but the continued "effort to induce the Indian to farm his own lands, to become self-sustaining and take his place as a citizen along with the white settler." White residents of Flathead argued that Indians could not be "induced to buckle down to real hard work" because "the traditions of the past [were] hard to eradicate." Settlers certainly needed water to have a chance at success, but their protests were evidence of a keen ability to play the victim. They believed they—rather than the federal government—were "conquering" the West. *The Ronan Pioneer* asserted, "everybody is admonished at this time to stay with it, don't be a quitter, and perhaps some day the light may penetrate where all is darkness now."[34]

The *Pioneer* proved adept at conflating hardship, yet not all their complaints were unfounded. What the government—particularly the Reclamation Service—failed to understand was that the average homesteader arrived with only enough money to get started in agriculture. The irrigation projects drew white settlers who saw them as quick schemes to make a profit, or at least a living. Waiting years for water quickly eroded the meager funds the settler brought with him. Developing a farm—building homes, fences, barns, and preparing the land for agriculture—often took all of a homesteader's savings. Credit offered one solution, but few had any collateral. It is no wonder that these people blamed the Reclamation Service, congress, and the "red tape" bound to irrigation. By late 1913, a few of the more hard-up abandoned the project. However, many who ventured to Flathead had both staying power and the means to take up more tribal lands. Secretary Lane supported these ventures, arguing "Idle Indians upon idle lands...must lead to the sale of the lands, for the pressing populations of the West will not long look upon resources unused without strenuous and effective protests." If the government could not induce the Flathead to work their irrigated lands, whites would become the beneficiary.[35]

The Interior Department's loyalty to either Indians or settlers never achieved consistency. In 1911, the BIA sent an appraisal commission to Flathead to reevaluate the 1904 assessment, and to examine tracts where the value of timber exceeded the use of land for farming or grazing. The commission classified most as timberland, closing it to homesteaders. Yet, a "misunderstanding" between the Indian and General Land Offices resulted in the approval of many filings. White settlers, believing themselves outside the bounds of Indian Office authority, sold timber rights on land they settled. Officials meant to use this timber, along with other forest assets, to fund irrigation. The BIA arbitrarily set a date when it believed the Land Office had due knowledge that the lands were classified as timber. Anyone filing prior to that time retained a preference right, but those filing after that date had their claims rejected. Commissioner Cato Sells concluded, "If such

a limit is not set hundreds of 'squatters' will go upon the timber lands...
and great confusion and expense to the United States and the Indians will
result."[36]

In 1914, the Indian Office sent William Ketcham to analyze the
situation. Whites continued to squat on timberlands that they desired to
clear for farms, and to settle lands within waterpower and reservoir sites or
lands reserved for Indian allotments, despite the rejection of their entries.
A new appraisal of the lands resulted in disparate values. Tracts originally
valued at ten cents to $7 an acre now had a value of $1 to $30; thus, a settler
who made entry at the time of the first appraisal could no longer afford the
purchase price.[37] Indians had a just claim for the higher price, while settlers
had a just claim to the initial price. For Ketcham, reservation settlement
foreshadowed a "time in no distant future" when whites would own the
majority of tribal property and the Indians would be landless and unable
to support themselves. He resolved, "The timber lands on this reservation,
if properly conserved and utilized, offer a partial remedy." The solution
was not in the conservation of forests, but, rather, in their removal and sale
to make way for irrigated agriculture and pastures for Indian stockmen.
Ketcham had the Indians' welfare in mind, but he saw their subsistence in
quickly and cheaply "disposing of the timber."[38]

Ketcham's conclusions about tribal timber tied directly into the
irrigation project. He argued that the failure to complete the project meant
that Indians would "suffer in common with the white settlers." A key
solution lay in leasing land to whites who had greater ability to finance the
agricultural endeavor. The cost of breaking the sod, leveling the land for
irrigation, and preparing the soil for crops represented an expense that only
a lessee with a long-term lease could bear. Moreover, as long as tribal lands
remained in Indian hands, the Flathead, under existing law, would have to
bear the cost of financing the irrigation project. The delays in selling land
had limited the amount available to reimburse the government. Ketcham
resolved that, via appropriations, the "government, and not the Indians, has
in reality been advancing the cost." The answer, Ketcham concluded, was
simple: sell more Flathead land to white settlers so that the value of water
rights—through construction and operation and maintenance costs—could
lessen the burden on the government.[39]

The question was who would receive, and use, the benefit of water and
who would pay for it? Ketcham confused the original intent of the project
with the reality. Indian Commissioner Sells explained it better: "On each of
these projects the work is largely done for the benefit of prospective owners
of surplus lands.... It will thus be seen that to all intents and purposes these
projects are [white] reclamation projects financed by Indian tribal property."

Flathead Reservation, early twentieth century.
(NA 8NS-75-97-221, box 7, #211)

Furthermore, officials admitted that the Indians—both those who used irrigation and those who would "receive nothing but an indirect benefit"— "were not consulted in this matter." Many Flathead had not wanted any part of the project, but merely the income from the increased land value that irrigation would supply. The chief engineer of the Indian Irrigation Service argued, "it does not seem fair and equitable that he should be called upon to finance a large scheme in which he has the minor interest, and in which, as an individual, he sometimes has no interest whatever." In short, unless the Indians wanted the water, they "should not be required to finance it."[40]

Frederick H. Abbott, secretary of the Board of Indian Commissioners, seconded these conclusions in his "Brief on Indian Irrigation." Abbott maintained that the primary problem on the projects had been that the Indians had no voice in the expenditure of their funds. Commissioner Sells tersely replied, "We do not agree that a voice on the part of the Indians as to construction and operation of irrigating systems is a fundamental principle necessary to be observed in handling these matters, as they involve questions of great economic importance and require the consideration of trained minds."[41] He also cited Indians' failure to utilize irrigated lands, pointing to the 1,088 acres used at Flathead out of the 38,000 possible. Yet, Abbott argued, lack of use could not "be charged to the indolence of the Indians," bur rather the failure of the government to consult with the tribe, explain their individual interest in the expenditure of tribal money, and show them the "dollars and cents" benefit.[42]

Regardless, the Indian and Reclamation Bureaus continued along the same path. In fact, Director Newell promoted irrigation construction that worked "towards evening up and bringing more of the white lands under cultivation by irrigation." While the question of what was best for the Flathead still generated much "food for thought," many agreed with Superintendent Morgan when he concluded, "what is good for the white man is good for the Indians." If whites could find ways to make a living through farming on the project, then so should Indians. However, Morgan ignored that although the Reclamation Service gradually put more land under ditch, the system still could not meet the demands for water. Water users cultivated 17,000 irrigated acres in 1915, but Indians only worked 1,500. Indians leased most of their irrigated lands, taking the better profit from renting, and chose to dry farm close to 39,000 acres.[43] Instead of food crops, the Flathead primarily grew hay to feed livestock. Mixed-bloods did most of the farming and stockraising, leaving full-bloods "worse off physically and financially than the same class were twenty-five years ago." The irrigation project encompassed close to 75,000 acres, and thus by subtracting the 17,000 acres actually irrigated, it was apparent that water flowed only through a small number of the ditches. *The Ronan Pioneer* complained that the "poor suckers who came to the Flathead five years ago...believing they had the world by the tail and...have lived on the hope that the next season the United States government would fulfill its promise and give them water" continued to be disappointed.[44]

Controversy over funding produced important changes on the Flathead Project. For many years, the main problem seemed to be that the congressional "appropriation committee [was] not very friendly to Montana or the west." Other complaints blamed poor use of funding, or as white settlers argued, "that procrastination, that vilest thief of all, has eaten the better portion of the funds and left the homesteader, who must ultimately pay the freight, high and dry." Interior Department bureaucracy contributed to the inefficiency. Political infighting between Interior Secretary Lane and Reclamation Director Newell resulted in Newell's dismissal, his replacement by Arthur P. Davis, and the reorganization of the Reclamation Service. Lane strove to put irrigation work on a "more sound and organized basis" through more efficient expenditure of funds and assurances of reimbursement.[45]

Pressure from the Comptroller of the U.S. Treasury forced the Interior Department to eliminate the red tape involved in financing its endeavors.[46] It put the Reclamation Service on an "appropriation basis." It could no longer front funding to the BIA, instead requiring that all irrigation work have proper insurance of congressional appropriations, as well as definite plans for reimbursement. Reclamation Service officials wanted to eliminate indebtedness from the Indian Irrigation Projects, and thus make sure that the Indian Office supplied money for construction in advance of the work actually being done.[47]

While these changes absolved the Reclamation Service of any financial obligation, it also meant that the Indian Office needed to ensure higher congressional appropriations so that work on the ground could continue in an efficient manner. The situation required the BIA to take a more active role in promoting the irrigation work as projects for Indians. Yet seeking larger support from congress meant an attempt to eliminate the "old scheme," whereby "Indian funds were hypothecated for all the expenses of irrigation construction." Because much of the irrigation benefit went to white-owned lands, the plan for funding proposed higher obligations on the part of white water-users. With the aid of Montana Senator Henry L. Meyers, these changes in policy achieved appropriations of $687,000 and $750,000 for work on the Flathead Project in 1916 and 1917, respectively. The shift in approach implied that the cost of construction would be borne by water-users, "Indian and white men alike, without discrimination, according to the benefits received by each." It also meant that more of the money from the sale of tribal lands, rather than financing irrigation, would be distributed as per capita payments, and the BIA hoped, contribute to Indian "prosperity and self-support."[48]

Federal officials expected this financial dueling to put Indian irrigation work on a sounder basis. However, since the inception of the Flathead Project, homesteaders had complained about the uncertainty of the final costs for construction. Knowing the final amount to be charged for irrigating a tract of land could mean the difference between a successful farming enterprise or debt and failure. Farmers wanted assurance that the final costs of construction, operation, and maintenance would not exceed their net profit. The ambiguity of final costs created a "money tightness" that impeded the sale of surplus tribal property. A settler hesitated to buy land without knowing the future liabilities attached to it.[49]

Many Indians were "dissatisfied with the way Uncle Sam [was] handling the reclamation work." Appearing before the Senate Committee on Indian affairs in 1917, a tribal delegation made a "violent and virulent attack on the Reclamation service and the Flathead reclamation project, claiming it was a fraud and a failure, that the Indians do not want it, that the white settlers do not want it, and that everybody wants it discontinued and chopped off right where it is." They charged "fraud, mismanagement, wastefulness, and extravagance," claiming Indians raised good crops without the project. The delegation had a valid point. Out of 2,980 farms on the reservation, only 303 used irrigation. Indians cultivated nearly 34,000 acres, but irrigated a mere 1,500. The 1915 crop season was the "Banner Year in the History of Western Montana," and though 1916 proved less productive, the Indians reportedly had a "ready demand for whatever grain they wished to dispose of." Of course, World War I inflated prices with demand. Regardless, both Indian and white farmers achieved more agricultural success than ever before.[50]

Statistics showed other important, and alarming, trends. Indians leased nearly 25,000 irrigated acres, or 95 percent of the total, to whites. Despite settlers' continued vitriol against the Reclamation Service, they benefited from irrigation. In fact, much of the ink that spilled from *The Ronan Pioneer* revealed the duplicitous nature of Flathead's non-Indian community. The editors called tribal protests against reclamation "worked up propaganda," claiming the Flathead had no justification for dissatisfaction. For white settlers, World War I inspired a newfound enthusiasm for patriotism, loyalty to government enterprise, and thus to irrigated agriculture. High wheat prices increased the acreage put into cultivation, while a new rail line between the towns of Dixon and Polson offered easier access to markets. Future prospects seemed brighter than ever, particularly for the industrious white farmer.[51]

Animosity between white settlers and Indians always existed at Flathead, but the angst began to reach new heights. As a direct result of tribal protests—or "Indian propaganda" as the *Pioneer* put it—congress reduced the irrigation appropriation for 1918 from $750,000 to $375,000. Superintendent Theodore Sharp contended that agitation against the project came from a coterie of "self-seekers" among the Indians. However, in defense of the Flathead, Sharp raised a vital, and often unrecognized, point. While some claims made by the tribe were "misleading," they had "good reason to complain" because the Reclamation Service had appropriated their property for reservoir sites without paying for the land; the Indians wisely utilized the Reclamation Service's line of reasoning about repayment to argue that reimbursement worked both ways. After all, if most of the reclaimed land was, or would become, the "property of white land owners," then justice would have to come through other means.[52]

*The "Moody Cases," Water Rights, and Irrigation Charges*

Conflict on the Flathead Irrigation Project came to a head in the 1920s. With an economic downturn in the years after World War I, disputes over water, and who had a right to profit from that resource, amplified the bitterness between Indians and whites and between Indians and the government. The animosity can be traced through the actions of C. J. Moody, Flathead Irrigation Project Supervisor from 1924 to 1933. Moody was a disciple of the idea that water would remake the West. His dedication to that principle obscured that prospects of development rode just as much on the interests of people as on the use of natural resources.[53]

The series of trials that made up the "Moody Cases" hinged on water rights. To begin to understand what happened during Moody's tenure as project supervisor, it is necessary to begin with complaints made by a Flathead delegation to Washington in 1919. The debate that began there led to the end of the Reclamation Service's involvement in irrigating Indian lands, and ultimately to the demise of the founding principles behind the Indian Irrigation Projects. On July 12, 1919, an obviously agitated E. B. Meritt, Assistant Commissioner of Indian Affairs, wrote Superintendent Sharp expressing concern over statements made to him by the delegation. The Indians alleged that the irrigation project had destroyed "certain old irrigation ditches" built by them prior to the entrance of the Reclamation Service. Meritt continued, "The [Indian] Office understands that the new system has appropriated certain old water rights of the Indians and has utilized or interfered with some of the ditches, but it also is under the impression that in every such case the Indian concerned has been cared for under the new project."[54]

The situation not only threatened the possibility of reimbursement to the government, but the Reclamation Service's rights to the waters of the reservation. The BIA formed a committee—including Sharp, a Reclamation Service engineer, and a tribal member—to investigate the situation. They concluded that old ditches existed, the owners had valid water rights, and the government should not interfere with them in any way. More significantly, if an allottee elected to exchange his water right for one in a new project ditch, the committee advised, he should be entitled to a paid-up water right of one hundred percent of the cost of construction but that he should pay operation and maintenance charges. However, they continued, if the government destroyed the old ditches then an individual "should be entitled to a paid-up water right to the extent of one hundred per cent of the cost of production *with no charge for operation and maintenance.*" These recommendations threatened the entire integrity of the Flathead Project.[55]

The Moody Cases began with *Lulu Allard v. C. J. Moody and the United States Reclamation Service.* In 1921, Allard alleged that Polson Lateral A, of the Reclamation Service's project, interfered with ditches her family constructed on their property years before. The Reclamation Service countered that Allard had applied for use of Polson Lateral B, and by so doing, agreed to water rental charges and the relinquishment of rights to the Allard ditches. Furthermore, the Reclamation Service contended, a restraining order to stop the operation of Lateral A would furnish no relief to Allard, but "cause injury to a large number of worthy people, both Indian and White, who have taken lands under this irrigation system for the purpose of making homes for themselves and their children and who have equal rights to this water with the plaintiff." Allard's use of old ditches hinged on rights to the waters of Big Creek, and if the court decided in her favor, the Reclamation Service would have to purchase her water right at great expense to the Flathead Project or abandon the Polson Lateral A system. And, as Moody concluded, the case raised the issue of whether the Reclamation Service could charge Indians for construction, operation, and maintenance of the project, "which matter is now being agitated by the Indians of this vicinity and which, based on early treaties, is a matter which possibly may be decided in favor of the Indians."[56]

U.S. Federal District Court Judge George Bourquin, long a defender of Indian rights, disagreed with the Reclamation Service's position. The Allard case represented "one of many in the same status" on the reservation. Reclamation Service officials correctly surmised that the judgment in the case would be "far reaching as affecting all the rights which [the Reclamation Service] claimed" for the Flathead Project, and threatened to derail all existing and future plans. The series of suits based on Indian water rights not only had "great importance" for Flathead, but provoked

Flathead Reservation, early twentieth century.
(NA 8NS-75-97-221, box 7, #214)

questions about irrigation on all Indian lands. The Moody cases involved Indians' prior treaty rights to water and the disposition of non-Indian water rights. In the notable case of *Winters v. United States* of 1908, the Supreme Court decided that Indians had a prior right to reservation waters to meet all their needs before serving the demands of whites. In *United States v. Buchanan*, a 1919 case involving Flathead, Bourquin decided likewise. However, conflict increasingly focused on the water rights of non-Indians who purchased property from Indian allottees who had treaty rights to water on that land. At issue was whether the transfer of land also included a conveyance of paid up water rights, and thus the elimination of obligations to pay project charges. The whole venture of Indian irrigation rode on the outcome of these questions. In short, would the Indian Irrigation Projects prove cost effective, or become government-sponsored welfare for both Indians and whites? The resolution of the Moody Cases—to a greater extent than the *Winters* case—could possibly determine the whole issue of water rights in the West and thus the prospects of agricultural development and success for millions of Americans.[57]

Debates over the "right" versus "privilege" to water created great conflict on the Flathead Reservation. What Indian Commissioner Charles H. Burke termed a "misunderstanding," most white settlers saw as fact. Purchasers of Indian allotments believed the price included "paid-up" water rights because ads for sale said nothing about reimbursement. In large part, that obscurity was intentional, a means to dispose of surplus lands as quickly as possible, but the mistake can also be partly chalked up to oversight. In 1921, Burke instructed all reservation superintendents to make clear on advertisements that the purchase of allotments also carried additional irrigation charges, and he requested that purchasers sign an agreement acknowledging their obligations. Serious doubts existed as to the means the government utilized to encourage white settlement at Flathead. The Interior Secretary admitted that the department had committed many mistakes, often issuing invitations that were "overly enthusiastic and painted the beauties and advantages of some of our projects in gorgeous colors." Irrigated agriculture at Flathead, however, made settlers confront a "stern reality" that frequently led to "disenchantment." The settler, the secretary concluded, "learned that homemaking means hard work and in many instances hardship." The decline of wartime demand produced a "general depression of business and farming interests" that only added to the anxiety over water.[58]

Confusion about non-Indian obligations contributed to mistakes in administering Indian use of irrigation. In direct defiance of policy, C. J. Moody refused to provide water to Indians who did not pay charges, though BIA regulations allowed accounts to be delinquent for up to one year. Moody responded, the Indians "are probably more interested in discrediting the value of irrigation and the work on the Flathead Project by the Reclamation Service than they are in the proper development of the Indian lands." The situation represented a failure to communicate—both between Moody and the Flathead and between Moody and the Reclamation Service. Moody contended that he did not practice "discrimination" against Indians in the use of water, yet his decisions revealed a growing conviction about Indian irrigated agriculture. As the Interior Secretary put it, "In so far as the Indian himself is directly concerned I can not say that the reclamation projects have proven a glowing success." He continued, "The Indians upon the reservations are not, as a general thing, tillers of the soil. I have never seen the fact commented upon, but it is worthy of note." This observation contradicted thirty years of Indian policy. Increasingly, government officials believed that tribal lands had much less, or no, "productive value," unless they were in the hands of white men. More and more, officials applied the same reasoning to irrigation projects.[59]

Nevertheless, the Reclamation Service touted the great changes, and thus development potential, it brought to Flathead through irrigation. The *Reclamation Record*—mouthpiece for the service—informed the public that by supplying the "life-giving fluid" of water, the Reclamation Service made it possible for the "hand of enterprise" to bring the outdated use of tribal lands into a modern era. The "pioneering days of the Flathead are over; we are on our way," exclaimed the *Record*, and that future had little to do with Indians. Agricultural development and speculation went hand in hand. For instance, one land company advertised 30,000 acres for sale at low prices, but when new settlers arrived the company tripled the selling price. "After waking from the dream of a large increase in farm population," Moody commented, "the people of the valley thank their lucky stars that the land company was not able to make sales at the prices asked," as it would have only added more "dissatisfied farmers." Indians continued to agitate against reclamation. In 1922, the Solicitor for the Interior Department rendered an opinion that it was unjust to charge them the same price as whites for the project, while taking thousands of acres of tribal land for reservoirs without payment. The department instructed Flathead Superintendent Charles E. Coe to appraise these lands in order to compensate the tribe. Little action was taken.[60]

Despite this contemplated concession, the Reclamation Service would not acquiesce in regard to water rights. Upon determining that the Flathead Project did not need the water from all the rivers on the reservation to fulfill the Indians' treaty rights, officials suggested that the "surplus waters" be sold to non-Indians. According to the Reclamation Service's logic, treaties only reserved the necessary amount of water to "properly irrigate" their land, all other water being surplus. However, the BIA contended that treaty rights reserved all water to the Indians for existing *and* future purposes. This debate rested on continuing questions about the old ditches built by Indians. The Indian Office maintained that individual water rights to streams on the reservation were, "without question, as good as water rights under works constructed for the Indians by the Government." In short, "surplus waters" did not mean any water not used by the Reclamation Service; rather, Indian rights included all water under the Flathead Project, individually-owned ditches, and all required water to irrigate land even if it was not currently "under constructed or proposed works of the general project."[61]

Relying on the *Winters* decision, the Indian Office argued that all actual and potential needs of the Indians must be met before water could be considered "surplus" and meted out to non-Indians. In effect, the BIA accused the Reclamation Service of attempting to subvert federal law and without congressional authority, and utilizing Montana state laws to disregard the amount of water needed by Indians in favor of whites. In turn, the Reclamation Service argued that it was by no means "certain that the conclusion in the Winter's case necessarily [applied] to the case of the Flathead Indians." They contended that *Winters* proceeded "upon the theory that it was the policy of the Government and the desire of the Indians to become a pastoral and civilized people." That argument relied on the 1855 Hellgate Treaty. The Reclamation Service claimed that the treaty did not mention any Flathead Indian water rights, but merely reserved "the right of taking fish in all the streams running through or bordering the reservation." With no mention of a "claim to water for irrigation purposes," the Reclamation Service considered the whole matter a closed case. Assistant Director Morris Bien concluded, "we should not acquiesce in this attitude of the Indian Office in regard to any reservation [for water] where the language of the treaty does not contain a reservation looking to agricultural purposes."[62]

The Reclamation Service based its assumptions on misinterpretations of the law. It assumed that reserved water rights were "inconsistent with the use of all water for fishing" as purportedly written in treaties. The Reclamation Service presumed that the Flathead had not lived up to their end of the bargain by not becoming diligent "agricultural people." In effect, their supposed lackluster performance as irrigation farmers exonerated the Reclamation Service in its attempts to abrogate water rights and pass on the surplus to whites. At least one Reclamation Service employee disagreed, arguing the Flathead allotment act never mentioned water and Indians never consented to allotment. Thus, Indian water rights remained as they were prior to allotment. He explained, "This project is an Indian one, and does not come under the laws applicable to the Reclamation Service"; the Reclamation Act could not be used to deny Indians' water rights.

The allotment act of 1904, as amended in 1908, included wording based on the conclusions in the *Winters* decision, and thus it seemed that existing law entitled the Indians to "every drop of water."[63] Whether the Indians became successful at farming had no relevance; in fact, because water had other uses besides agriculture, the Flathead Project itself had little bearing on Indian rights. Reclamation Service officials misread history, ignoring that the 1855 treaty with the Flathead reserved all waters rising upon, flowing through, and bordering the reservation. Their arguments seemed like another Interior Department "smoke screen" to hide the "actual purpose" of reclamation policy.[64]

The sparring between the Reclamation and Indian bureaus on national Indian irrigation evidenced twenty years of hard feelings. Bickering began before workers removed the first shovel-full of dirt. As historian Donald Pisani has noted, the two bureaus were "uneasy allies" in their irrigation endeavor on tribal lands. Initially, in 1907, Secretary of the Interior James Garfield, finding it necessary to build irrigation projects for both Indians and whites, "conceived the idea that for efficiency and economy it would be desirable to combine the work." However, the Comptroller of the Treasury's decision in 1911 to put budgetary matters on a more organized basis threatened that cooperation. This initial conflict came down to money, and which bureau would front the money for Indian irrigation. Supposedly, rearranging the method of payment would provide "efficiency and economy," but all it really caused was increased inter-bureau animosity.[65]

Money, even greed, became the principal point of conflict. The question remained: who financed the projects and who benefited? Frederick Newell, while still the Reclamation Director in March of 1914, noted that the "persistent misunderstanding" that funds spent on the Indian Irrigation Projects benefited whites the most hampered positive construction progress. Newell asked that the Reclamation Service be relieved of further responsibility because the "difficulties and annoyance" were so great, that without "complete team play," the efforts at Indian irrigation were "likely to be in vain." The Comptroller's decision to put Reclamation on an "appropriation basis" resulted "in the tying up at all times" of hundreds of thousands of dollars for Flathead work, leaving the Reclamation Service in the black. The problem also stemmed from the BIA's failure to collect money to reimburse the Reclamation Service. By 1916, the Reclamation Service viewed the situation as an Indian Office endeavor "to shift the responsibility" for the project upon the Reclamation Service. It contended that Flathead was an "Indian project," while the Indian Office claimed it was a "general" white reclamation project. No one wanted the liability.[66]

The arguments in the offices at Washington were heard in congress and in the field. Montana Senator Henry L. Meyers put in overtime fighting for the project. By 1921, his exasperation had grown so great that he groused, "The opposition to it and the prejudice against it have been inconceivable and insurmountable. The obstacles have been innumerable and almost unconquerable. One thing after another continually arises to hamper effort and impede progress." Myers succeeded in getting appropriations of $750,000 in successive years prior to World War I. Funding dropped during the war and after hostilities ended the "great cry" in Washington was "cut everything to the bone" in order to reduce expenses and offset war debt. However, he continued, "The great stumbling block is and always has been in the Indian Bureau.... The present administration seems to be determined to make a record for economy, regardless of consequences." Myers blamed Commissioner Burke for taking a conservative stance on Indian irrigation and failing to promote its benefits. Myers had a point, but Burke's hesitancy also reflected the growing rift between the Indian and Reclamation Bureaus. Burke argued the "voluminous" legislation relating to Indian affairs,

Flathead Reservation, early twentieth century.
(NA 8NS-75-97-221, box 7, #216)

particularly irrigation, hampered effective management. He felt that as an increasing percentage of tribal land on the project passed into white ownership, the issue of irrigation required "closer supervision" to protect Indian interests. This required a "genuine and sympathetic understanding of the human side of the Indian, his limitations and aspirations." Giving charge of the endeavor to the Reclamation Service—"a bureau primarily charged with fostering the interests of the whites"—proved detrimental to the Flathead. Burke claimed that "protecting and advancing the welfare of the Indians" superseded a policy of quicker construction that tended to neglect those issues.[67]

Interesting contradictions existed to Burke's assertions. If the BIA wanted to wrest control of the Flathead Project from the Reclamation Service because it was not doing an efficient job of making the Indians self-supporting farmers, why did the BIA approve so many leases and sales of Indian allotments? The easy answer was that sales and leases of allotments provided income. However, leasing brought in short-term profit and those returns did little to make Indians into farmers. In turn, little evidence existed to verify the benign claims about helping Indians. Of the 56,310 irrigable acres on the reservation in 1921, the Flathead rented out over 30,000. Whites owned at least an additional 24,000 irrigated acres. Indians utilized a mere 1,760 irrigable, allotted acres. No wonder, as C. J. Moody reported, that there was "a constant agitation by certain members of the tribe against the Reclamation Service, representing that the Service is not fair with Indians."

The Flathead demanded the elimination of all construction charges against their lands. Also, few Indians had the capability of meeting the one-year deadline for payment of operation and maintenance charges—the fees to cover water delivery and repair of project structures. Reclamation Service officials argued that water should not be delivered to Indians who did not pay their bills. The Indian Office replied that such a penalty put an unfair "additional burden upon the Indian lands" that would prevent both the development of the Flathead and their farms. In the end, the bureaus agreed to defer the payments until 1923. White settlers also complained. As one irate settler put it, "Some are going back to dry farming simply because they can't raise the money to pay their water bills." The Reclamation Service's failure to announce the final amount of construction charges disqualified white farmers from taking advantage of the Federal Farm Loan Act, money they needed to finance agricultural development.[68]

In 1924, Interior Secretary Hubert Work transferred control of the Indian Irrigation Projects from the Reclamation Service to the Indian Office. From the beginning, the Reclamation Service acted in the capacity of a contractor, construction agent, and "legal advisor" for the BIA. At the outset, the Interior Department believed the Reclamation Service had better engineering skills, management ability, and the necessary equipment to construct the Indian Projects. The 1902 reclamation act outfitted the Reclamation Service with the necessary means to build and operate large irrigation works, and thus made the Reclamation Service more competent for the Indian Projects. By 1924, the amount of work on Indian irrigation had been reduced to an extent that eliminated the necessity of Reclamation Service involvement. The Indian Office purportedly could now handle the work.[69]

Secretary Work asked Commissioner Burke to justify the transfer. He began with the argument that the work on tribal lands required constant contact with Indians. The task seemed better suited to the BIA than the Reclamation Service, a bureau "not acquainted with Indian characteristics and habits." The projects entailed more than irrigation, but the improvement of Indians. Irrigation construction provided employment. That goal was a "means of education," Burke contended, and one "of vast importance in reaching the ultimate goal for which we are striving with respect to the Indian's future welfare." The Reclamation Service, a bureau not conceived for the purpose of looking after Indians' interests, "would not and could not render this invaluable service." The BIA assisted tribes to properly cultivate their lands with irrigation. As another "educational phase" of the work, it did not correspond with the abilities of the Reclamation Service. Burke also claimed that the Indian Office could do the same work as the Reclamation Service at a smaller overall cost. All of Burke's justifications were questionable. He contended that the great cost of the projects, under Reclamation Service authority, did not produce any marked degree of success. Laying blame for high costs and paltry results on the Reclamation Service neglected the role the BIA played in planning and financing Indian irrigation.[70]

Burke's suppositions also ignored the Indian Office's role on the ground. For instance, if the goal of Indian education intertwined with irrigation, why did officials consistently approve the leasing of great amounts of irrigable acreage? Why did whites own such a large proportion of irrigated property? Why did so many Flathead claim they were treated unfairly? Why were there so few Indians utilizing irrigation? The Reclamation Service certainly played a role. However, the BIA always had the bigger hand in making decisions affecting Indian irrigation. And now, with full responsibility for the Flathead Project, the Indian Office would be confronted with the problems of irrigation and its own hypocrisy.

Contrary to hopes, transferring the Indian Projects from the Reclamation Service to the BIA did not mean closer observance of the needs and desires of the Flathead. The most obvious issue was the contradiction inherent in the Indian Irrigation Projects, namely, whites often benefited to a larger extent than Indians. *The Ronan Pioneer* offered a superb example. In 1923, the newspaper described how one enterprising white farmer was able to "make things go." Lars Beck began at Flathead with eighty acres, a few cows, a plow, and a hoe. Between 1917 and 1923, Beck progressively added more acreage, livestock, and better equipment. In his seventh year at Flathead, Beck raked in over $2,800 in profit and expected $3,000 the following year. His success allowed him to buy a Ford, a manure spreader, a washing machine, and other agricultural implements without going into debt. The *Pioneer* mused that there wasn't "the least likelihood that Lars Beck will die a millionaire, but he is extracting a very comfortable living for himself and his very fine family." Presses across the nation ran the story. Beck represented the pinnacle of achievement, indicated what the "diligent" farmer could produce, and supplied the "best boost" possible to the potential of irrigated agriculture at Flathead.[71]

Lars Beck's fame as an industrious farmer belied the reality of making a living on the Flathead Project. Beck may have symbolized success, but he was more illusion than icon. One only needs to consider the case of homesteader Edith Siner to discolor the glowing picture of triumph. In 1913, Siner, her husband, and six children began with ninety-one acres— more than Beck. The Siners planted and fenced an orchard, built a house, and dug a cellar and well. They cleared sixty acres of sagebrush and put it in cultivation. In the first two years, the family raised a subsistence crop. "Then," Siner noted, "came the dry years. We stayed on the place 7 years trusting the Government for water, as they had promised, as we fully expected to make this our home. But no water came." By 1924, Siner's land had little or no value. The Siner's spent $1,690 improving the land. Now, they could not sell or rent it. She concluded, "We certainly would never have taken the land if we had thought we would have never gotten water. But we trusted the Government." Siner's case was not atypical. The mayor of Missoula wrote Montana Senator John M. Evans: "Nearly one half of the farms are deserted and a large part of the farmers who remain are so heavily involved in debt that I can not see how they can ever recover." Most farmers were four years or more in arrears on these payments, and the government had applied the "Shylock" interest rate of one percent to delinquent accounts. Settlers blamed the Indian Office, Reclamation Service, Interior Department, Land Office, and whoever else fell under their swath of criticism. It was a "physical impossibility" for a settler and his family to take up a forty and wait years for water. Any settler could recount "stories of sacrifices, martyrdoms, and tragedies" because the government had "not kept faith."[72]

While white settlers demanded "justice," others questioned the viability of the irrigation project. Some farmers did not get the water they needed, but records indicated that they did not fully use the available water supply. In 1925, whites owned 29,000 irrigable acres and leased 32,000, while Indians used a mere 2,832 irrigated acres. Of the 61,000 irrigated acres worked by whites, they raised crops on 36,528 acres with a product value of $695,800. Apparently, the government had a point about the failure to utilize all irrigable land. Moreover, the Flathead Tribal Council opposed further appropriations for the project, claiming that there was "now water enough to justify everyone concerned." They believed that further construction would only bring more hardship, because much of the acreage under ditches had a lien greater than the actual value of the land. Interior Secretary Work argued his department believed in "furthering federal reclamation," but was not willing to allow reclamation "to continue to ride recklessly to its own ruin." Work had grown exasperated with settlers who, instead of "having a sense of gratitude to the government for what it has done for them," expressed "disappointment and bitterness." To ensure the future of reclamation, Work contended, the government must "first reclaim reclamation." The Interior Department needed to "restore lost confidence in its government representatives, re-establish the enthusiasm brought on to projects by settlers, and discredit those who live by farming the farmers."[73]

Work's goal of putting reclamation "on an efficient basis" disregarded the human—particularly, the Indian—side of the story. Prior to 1916, the plan for irrigation not only contemplated the sale of tribal property to support the endeavor, but consistently ignored Indians' lack of interest in utilizing irrigation. That year, Interior directed that repayment for charges would be borne by both Indians and whites according to the amount of irrigable acreage they owned. This change encumbered Indian property with a lien for all the water they had ever used; for those Indians that used water, the charges amounted to a back payment for six years. Few could afford to pay. In the meantime, many Indians "gave up in despair and quit farming." The Reclamation Service collected some of the charges by debiting funds accruing to the Indians' credit from land and timber sales and other per capita payments. The supposed debts piled up, reaching an impossible figure by the mid-1920s. By then, Indian hostility towards reclamation reached a boiling point. They contended that because the government had issued their patents to land prior to the inception of the irrigation project, and also because patents contained no lien for water, that the government could not impose such a debt. Indians also argued that they shouldn't be forced to pay for projects they had no say in approving and that had been imposed upon them. Work ignored the claims and ordered Superintendent Coe to collect a fifty-cent per acre charge. His action not only worked "hardships" on the Indians that hindered their ability to farm, but often prevented them from leasing their lands.[74]

Much confusion existed "due to a lack of uniformity of laws applying to Indians' irrigation projects." By 1925, the government had spent nearly $5.5 million on the Flathead Project, little of which had been repaid. The policy for collecting charges continued to befuddle settlers and Indians alike. Congress appointed a committee, led by Congressman Louis C. Cramton of Michigan, to investigate irrigation on tribal lands. Many Flathead settlers found Cramton disingenuous, criticizing a speech he made for being "in the form of a dictator addressing his slaves." They attacked Work for halting reclamation progress. They belittled President Calvin Coolidge who agreed to delays on the basis that American farmers had produced a surplus that brought them inadequate returns. White settlers dismissed Coolidge's reasoning, and through the *Pioneer* threatened "to make trouble for the administration." In house debates during 1926, congressmen "assailed" Secretary Work, Reclamation Director Elwood Mead, and the Indian Office "for failing to carry out reclamation laws as interpreted by Congress." The house assault was duplicitous because congress shared the blame for failing to appropriate sufficient amounts for Indian irrigation. In the end, congress approved $575,000 for Flathead work in fiscal year 1927. Ironically, *The Ronan Pioneer* credited Cramton for the substantial funding.[75]

The battle did not end with the congressional appropriation. The Flathead Tribal Council filed suit on the grounds that the proposed irrigation plan was "detrimental to the Indians," and the court issued a restraining order against the project. Their complaint focused on conditions of the appropriation act requiring the formation of irrigation districts prior to the disbursal of money. When irrigators formed an irrigation district they immediately fell under state law and the land would be subject to state taxes. As federal wards, Indians had no obligation to the state, but the requirements of the act placed them in the possible predicament of "unjust taxation." In the end, the U.S. District Court of Montana dismissed the suit, irrigators formed the irrigation districts, and as a further requirement, drew up contracts outlining the repayment of construction charges. That same month, in an op-ed piece, Indian Commissioner Burke wrote, "That the American Indian is dying out is a common fallacy.... One of the many causes contributing to the rise in general well-being of these, the only real 'native' Americans, is land reclamation." While it was true that the Indians weren't dying out, the fallacy was that reclamation contributed to the "well-

Flathead Reservation, early twentieth century.
(NA 8NS-75-97-221, box 7, #215)

being" of Indians. In a report on the Flathead Project, the Board of Indian Commissioners asserted that the only possible reason to continue would be "solely to provide irrigated lands for the Indians themselves." While Burke gave vague generalities, the Board provided rationalizations—in fact, the original theoretical basis of Indian irrigation—about self-support. Both offered idealism, and both had failed to learn the lessons of limitation taught by twenty years of work on the Flathead Irrigation Project.[76]

The Moody Cases were as much about repayment as water rights. In 1928, the Interior Department appropriation act required the collection of all charges for water on a per acre basis. Any unpaid amount constituted a first lien on irrigated lands. The legislation dictated payment by Indians and whites alike, regardless of any claim to water rights. If an Indian used water, he must pay; if a purchaser bought Indian land, he must pay; if a non-Indian leased Indian land, he must pay. Interior and the BIA took what seemed the most "rational step" to "protect" the government's investment, but the move was unrealistic and negligent. Applying a lien for unpaid charges only compounded Indians' difficulty in selling or leasing land. The Moody Cases centered on the argument that Indians had acquired rights to, built ditches for, and diverted water long before the federal project began.

Flathead Superintendent Coe could not collect the construction charges as mandated by the Interior Department. "The theory of collecting a minimum operation and maintenance to encourage or rather to force the use of water" neglected the condition of Indian farmers. Many refused to farm because of their dissatisfaction. Finally, Coe concluded, "The average Indian believes he is entitled to water without paying construction costs and I am inclined to believe he may be right."[77]

The issues at stake in the Moody Cases multiplied the difficulties of the irrigation project. Whatever the right of Indians to their old ditches, and thus to a "gratuitous" water right, much of that land had passed into white ownership. Whites claimed that the purchase carried the "paid-up right." To the consternation of the Indian Office, these settlers exercised their "private water rights" in a manner detrimental to the larger project. They simply took the water they needed and refused to pay for it. Because the private and project ditches overlapped each other, officials found it a "physical impossibility" to "fully measure or control all the water" used. The BIA could not properly apportion water under the project if they could not quantify the amount taken via private ditches. The dilemma over using and paying for water even caused Indian Commissioner Charles Rhoads to suggest returning the Flathead Project to Reclamation Service control. The government initially promised irrigation at a relatively low cost. Indians, as Montana Senator Burton K. Wheeler put it, felt "that the subsequent repudiation of such a declaration" did not show "very good grace on the part of the Government." Indians were "afraid of the costs" of irrigation and would not use the water. Instead of promoting progress, Superintendent Coe surmised, "Irrigation is the most serious obstacle to the Indian farmer on this reservation."[78]

*The Preston-Engle Report and the Survey of Conditions of Indians in the United States*

The Interior Department and its subsidiaries had made irrigation inimical to Indians. In 1929-30, all the problems came to a head in a series of damning investigations commissioned by congress.[79] One such report made by Porter J. Preston, a Reclamation Service engineer, and Charles Engle, a BIA engineer, obliterated all traces of idealism still existing about the Indian Irrigation Projects. Their most important criticism, though not new, was that most "Indian" projects had become "white" projects. On Flathead, Indians irrigated only 1.3 percent and whites the rest.[80] Preston and Engle surmised, because of "overoptimism, coupled with a desire to demonstrate the feasibility of a project and thus bring about its construction, there has been a surrender…to the inherent human tendency to minimize difficulties and swell the irrigable acreage" by including lands that could never be profitably used.[81]

Indians' lack of use was astounding. The report explained how Indian projects became white projects: "The continual decrease in the acreage farmed by Indians is the natural and logical result of the leasing system, and the leasing system in turn is the inevitable result of the allotting system." Leasing was also the natural outcome of the requirement that Indians use the land to secure their water rights and make money to pay water charges. With its easier income, leasing also prevented Indians from becoming farmers. Or, as the report put it, leasing was "a virtual return to the ration system," whereby "the irrigation system, instead of being a benefit to the Indians, is a curse." The ideology of irrigation presumably focused on making Indians into self-supporting farmers. However, rather than "educating" the Indian, the projects actually taught the Reclamation and Indian Bureaus "that the building of dams and canals does not of itself create irrigated agriculture."[82]

Instead of creating Indian farmers, irrigation offered wage labor constructing canals. Rather than promoting Indian advancement, projects largely served as "welfare activity." The report made clear that it was hopeless and unjust to expect Indians to pay irrigation charges. Forced reimbursement often caused them "to slow up or to lose interest in the development and use of his irrigable land." Many Indians saw legislation requiring Indian payment, and Indian Projects in general, as "a scheme to dispossess them of their lands" by assessing irrigation charges to the point where the cost exceeded the value of their land. Whites also criticized repayment, arguing it was "taxation without representation" and the government treated them "as foreigners without rights."[83]

The Preston-Engle Report singled out the Flathead Irrigation Project for its great size and expense. The total construction cost of the project had reached $5.2 million, while operation and maintenance amounted to nearly $800,000. Irrigators had repaid a mere 1.5 percent of the cost of construction, but the government had managed to collect forty percent of the operation and maintenance charges. The project cost based on the amount of land actually irrigated was $156.07 per acre. To make sound business sense, the agricultural income per acre had to match that figure. Yet the average white farmer produced a per acre crop value between seventeen and eighteen dollars, while Indians generated less than fifteen dollars. Of course, if irrigators refused to pay the project charges, "economic feasibility" really had no meaning at all.[84]

How farmers used irrigation was a vital indicator of the Flathead Project's value. In the mid-1920s, 116 Indian families cultivated eleven hundred irrigated acres; if distributed evenly, this meant that each family, in the year of highest usage, only raised crops on fifteen irrigated acres. In 1924, each of the above families took in about $258, or for a family of four, about $65 per person. Two years later, families only made about $58 each. Most Indian families likely had more than four people, including parents, children, grandparents, and various relatives that depended on the family for support. To be fair, it must be noted that many Indian families dry-farmed and raised livestock, making enough to feed and clothe themselves. But, the point is that Indians did not use the irrigation project.[85]

Whites did much better than Indians. On leased and owned land, whites cultivated approximately 33,000 irrigated acres. Crop production generated a yearly average income of $600,000, or $481 for each farmer. While not a great deal, it was not bad considering what Indians made. Naturally, the income fluctuated from year to year. In the late 1920s, arguments about reimbursement and the payment of increasing operation and maintenance charges drastically reduced the amount of land that whites leased for irrigated agriculture. Instead, many whites turned to leasing Indian lands for purposes besides irrigation, such as stockraising.[86]

Preston and Engle blamed the Indian Office for the failures of Indian irrigation, alleging that its officials "evinced a tendency to create an alibi by claiming that they were not in any way responsible either for the selection of the projects or conduct of the work" because that was the Reclamation Service's job. The argument that the BIA was better suited for protecting Indian rights had "little merit" because the "large and well organized legal staff" of the Reclamation Service had better ability to defend Indians than the one attorney employed by the Indian Office. They recommended the return of larger Indian works, like Flathead, to Reclamation Service control.[87]

The downturn in leasing evidenced by the Preston-Engle Report revealed changing land values. In the late 1920s, whites gradually purchased more irrigated lands, choosing to secure their assets through ownership rather than risk losing money through irrigation charges on rented land. Alternatively, Indians increasingly chose dry-farming over irrigation. By 1928, a scant ten Indians families cultivated a total of 300 irrigated acres. Interior Secretary Roy O. West, responding to the report, acknowledged that the BIA had not kept up with the changing economic and social conditions on and near reservations, and its failure to adjust to new circumstances caused many of the problems of Indian administration. The growing white population of reservations not only purchased irrigable lands, but promoted advertising campaigns that brought in more whites wanting to "secure control" of irrigated Indian property. Indian policy, West admitted, had become anachronistic. Instead of admitting Indians' lack of interest in irrigation, officials claimed Indians "lacked aptitude and experience and that he might require a long, unprofitable apprenticeship, before he would become a skilled irrigation farmer." Aiming to make Indians into yeoman irrigation farmers, rather than visualizing other economic opportunities, created an Indian policy that was "inadequate to meet abuses" arising when land and water passed into white control.[88]

Despite all the confusion that seemed to flow from BIA bureaucracy, Indians' accounts about water on the Flathead Reservation made it perfectly clear that they did not misunderstand history. The statement of Albert Lemery, a member of the tribal council, to the Senate committee on Indian affairs in 1930, made this obvious. Lemery explained that the Flathead had once been ideal livestock country, but now, because of the "useless irrigation project," it was a "secondhand farming country." His experience showed that a combination of dry-farming and summer fallowing produced better crops that those raised "under the ditch," or as he stated, "the less water you use the better." The Flathead protested the project from the beginning and still opposed it. The land had been "practically confiscated by liens" for water charges, causing many Indians to abandon lands under the project without planting any crops. The charges had reached such a high sum that it proved impossible to raise enough crops to pay for the water, and the accumulated charges were more than the value of the land itself. Lemery argued that the project was "ruining the Indians and threatening the destruction of the Flathead Valley." He maintained that the treaty of 1855 confirmed the Flathead's ownership of the reservation and that included the water rights. Though the tribe had the water to begin with, the government came in and took over Flathead's private irrigation ditches, appropriated the water, tore up many of the old canals, built new ones, and "then they turned around and charged the Indians the same as anybody else for using water." The Flathead Project took all the old ditches plus the lands for new reservoir sites, but the government never "paid a cent for it." Quite clearly, Albert Lemery had the story of water on Flathead down pat.[89]

Marie Lemery testified that the government never consulted the Flathead on the project, but they did not want it and never agreed to it. The Indians protested—in person, in writing, and via telegraph—because they believed they could not afford to pay water charges. However, she accused, the government paid no attention to the protests. The government offered them lies along with the irrigation. Lemery explained, "The Indians were told that it would increase the value of their land, and this is how it does— we bought an 80 several years ago for $3,500 and if we were to sell the same land to-day we could not get $1,500 for it." Moreover, she argued, "that is true of practically all the land under the irrigation project, and, so, instead of land increasing in value it has decreased." The whole argument that the "department in Washington" served as a guardian protecting Flathead interests was outright fabrication. She concluded that the irrigation system epitomized the general mismanagement of all the Flathead's affairs.[90]

Indian testimony fouled the water. The government did not understand, Moses Grenier commented, that the "Indians here are not farmers and I don't think they ever will be." Plus, the young people saw no future in agriculture. Octave Couture, a resident of the Jocko district, explained that, prior to the Reclamation Service project, about thirty-five Indians irrigated their farms from ditches they had built themselves. The government gave control of the ditches to the Indians as "consideration for making the treaty." But then, it came in and took the ditches, without payment, and built the project. The government promised "free water" as soon as Indians took allotments. Now, only two or three used irrigation because most "could not [both] make a living and pay for the water." As far as the system being a benefit to the Indians, Couture concluded, "it don't amount to nothing and they get no good of it." Henry Matt aptly summarized, the government stole the Indians' water "and all they got for it was stones."[91]

Indian testimony left much for the Indian Office to answer for. Chairman of the hearings, Burton K. Wheeler, put C. J. Moody in the

Flathead Reservation, early twentieth century.
(NA 8NS-75-97-221, box 7, #221)

hot seat. Wheeler accused the Flathead irrigation staff of building a huge project beyond the needs of farmers. Moody admitted that water had never been turned into more than fifty miles of ditches. Wheeler scoffed, "You mean…they were never used—in other words they [were] abandoned?" Showing great aptitude for twisted truth, Moody replied, "I prefer to say they are not used." Wheeler bantered, "As a matter of fact, the reason they are not being used is because all of the farmers along the ditch have moved away." Farmers also left because they did not get water in a timely fashion. Moody replied, "Yes, but you are not blaming us for that—we did not get the money." By then, congress had appropriated nearly six million dollars for the Indian Office to complete construction. Another vital issue focused on the inability of white farmers to meet the construction charges. Thus, the government extended the payment plan to forty years. Despite this leniency, Moody admitted, it would still prove impossible in the end for white irrigators to pay the costs for water.[92]

At the time of the Senate hearings, about three hundred Flathead owned land "under the ditch," but only ten percent used the water. Moody explained, "The biggest part of my work has been in connection with the Indians, trying to get them to irrigate." The real question was, out of the Indians actually using irrigation, how many actually made a sufficient living? Moody vaguely replied, "They are getting by." Even supposing that more began to use irrigation, their ability to make a living seemed impossible. If the government assessed the Flathead for construction charges, then at $100 per acre, very few would break even and most of them would be totally broken. To reconcile some of the failings, Wheeler surmised, "There will have to be a radical change won't there, more than there has been in the last 150 years that they have been here. Doesn't it mean that the Government will have to cancel these liens or take over the Indians' land?" Moody replied with a resigned "yes," the only possible answer lay in canceling all charges against the Indians.[93]

C. J. Moody came to symbolize all that was wrong with the Montana Indian projects. By the fall of 1931, twenty-five cases, involving at least one hundred Indian and white irrigators, had been filed against him on Flathead water issues as the agent of the Interior Department. Benjamin P. Harwood, legal counsel for the Indian Office, summarized the government's view: "It is clear that the suits would never have been brought if it were not for project irrigation charges, and that they were brought primarily for the purpose of avoiding payment of such charges." Yet this argument disregarded the issue of Indian treaty rights to water prior to federal appropriation. The plaintiffs—primarily whites who purchased Indian allotments—argued that their Indian predecessors built canals, diverted water, the old systems supplied all their needs, the government interfered by building project ditches, and without the intrusion they "would still be enjoying the original systems without payment of charges to anyone." They concluded that because such irrigation systems were "vested property appurtenant to their land," the government could not infringe in any way on that right.[94]

U.S. District Court Judge Bourquin concurred with the plaintiffs, concluding that anyone who acquired land served by the old ditches prior to the act of 1916—the legislation that required reimbursement for irrigation on Flathead—did not have to pay construction, operation, or maintenance charges. The decision rested on whether the plaintiffs were "in the project." Having concluded that ditches built in the 1890s were the "private property of the Indian allottees," no other decision in the case seemed just. The Interior Department appealed. If the government did not win it would vitally affect not only Flathead, but all Indian Irrigation Projects. As one official noted, it would "make impossible the collection of a very large amount of reimbursable money of the United States."[95]

In 1933, the BIA won the appeal on a technicality. The U.S. Circuit Court of Appeals dismissed nine of the Moody Cases because only the Interior Secretary had the authority to order the collection of water charges, but he was not named as a party to the suits. The government could not fully celebrate. Officials hesitated to accept victory considering the animus produced by the congressional investigations. In late October, Interior Secretary Harold Ickes asked the Attorney General to file counter-suits against the remaining plaintiffs involved in cases against Moody. Ickes wanted to discourage these irrigators from attempting to secure "benefits under the project without payment of their proportionate share of the annual costs." The suits aimed to foreclose on the lands of the claimants for unpaid water charges. However, Kenneth R. L. Simmons, legal counsel for the Indian Office, warned that while there might be legal grounds for foreclosure, the "matters should be settled by compromise." The BIA did not want enemies, but a clarification of reimbursement and water rights.[96]

The Indian Office sought three goals in the Moody litigation: it wanted to bring an end to all the lawsuits; it aimed to clarify and solve all the problems on water rights and the "enforcement of statutory liens for delinquent construction"; and it wanted to place the "project on a sound and workable basis" and "define the financial obligations" of all landowners. The appeal decided in favor of the government on the nine cases prompted new appeals on those nine, as well as fifty-five new suits. Unfortunately, Simmons reported, Bourquin was presiding in these cases and he "was very antagonistic to the government." The delays caused by the suits created "a staggering number of delinquencies," not due so much to the Great

Depression, but to landowners' doubts about the "legality of the assessments made against their lands by the government." In 1933 and 1934, with more than seven million dollars spent on the project, delinquency reached a rate near one hundred percent. A lien act of 1926 ensured collection of all charges since that time, however, considering decisions rendered by Bourquin, reimbursement of all previous charges seemed precarious.[97]

Though complex, these cases hinged on a few key issues. Irrigators saw the government charges as illegal, and many of the "substantial farmers" let the delinquencies add up "simply to bring the matter to a head and force" the government to determine the legality of the charges. The cases centered on the appropriation of water on Indian reservations. They involved not just the Flathead, but the precedent set by the *Winters* case. As Simmons put it, "There is no possibility of compromise. There is nothing to compromise. We are either right or they are right. They have a paid up water right or they have nothing." The Leavitt Act of 1932 seemed to justify relief of the charges for Indians, and some officials contended that the act contained an "implied invitation" to adjust charges for non-Indians.[98] The Indian Office replaced Moody with Henry Gerharz who concluded that "no possibility of collection" existed from the Flathead. Cancellation of the reimbursable charges was the only option. For all their drama, the Moody Cases ended in anti-climax. Indians had no responsibility for payment, but white water users did.[99]

Meanwhile, drought and depression reshaped irrigation at Flathead. In the arid conditions crops without irrigation failed, and crops with irrigation at best brought average returns. While whites continued to do fairly well, the battles over water had completely embittered Indians against irrigation. Only about one hundred and thirty Indians farmed, most choosing to raise livestock instead. By 1932, the "unhappy economic conditions" had severely handicapped the leasing of Indian lands, and many whites requested cancellation, reduction of rental prices, or the "acceptance of other considerations in lieu of cash" for farming land. In equal measure to the Preston-Engle Report, Senate hearings, and the Moody Cases, it was drought, depression, and the low price of farm products that remade Indian Irrigation Projects. Year by year, congress consistently deferred (sometimes only reduced) non-Indian payments for irrigation at Flathead. In 1932, legislation deferred Indians' future costs so long as they held title.[100]

Conditions also forced the Indian Office to address difficult questions. John Collier, at the time with the American Indian Defense Association, put pressure on the BIA to deal with the problems over tribal land used for irrigation. Officials had already acknowledged that the Reclamation and Indian Bureaus seized Indian property for reservoir sites without payment or rental. Superintendent Coe and C. J. Moody made an appraisal, and by giving the Indians no role in that assessment, demonstrated their "indifference to the tribal interests" and "contempt of tribal wishes." Moody, in his role as project engineer, did not play a disinterested role as he obviously wanted to procure the sites at a minimum price. Thus, Collier charged, it was "curious" that the Indian Office cut the value from the $100 per acre estimate in 1928 to $30 in a current appraisal. The "scheme" represented the "indefensible idea of awarding the value as of the time when the lands were forcibly taken" rather than the present value.[101]

When Collier became Commissioner of Indian Affairs in 1933, he began implementing policies to rectify, at least partially, some of the inequities in Indian irrigation. On BIA recommendation, congress continued to defer repayment for construction. In 1933, Interior Secretary Ickes canceled over $2 million of individual Indian debt for irrigation charges. While the Indians might not receive direct benefit from water, New Deal funds would provide other means of compensation. The Indian Irrigation Service utilized Emergency Conservation Work and Public Works funds to increase the pace of construction on the Flathead Project. The Indian Office instructed the service to give first preference to Indians in that work. In 1934, the BIA began reorganizing all its irrigation work for better economy, improved administration, and "closer cooperation." The plans proposed turning over operation and management of the projects to water users' associations—both Indian and non-Indian—the idea being, that upon completion, the water users would operate the projects "without further assistance." New Deal programs and funding, more than anything else, gave the final push to finish the Flathead Project. The New Deal would finish what had been left undone for over twenty years even though Indians had less and less incentive to farm and more and more incentive to find other forms of employment.[102]

While years of neglect and conflict still tainted many people's feelings about the government, use of the irrigation system—by whites—gradually increased. From 1934 to 1936, irrigation by white lessees and owners rose from 59,000 to 67,000 acres. Meanwhile, Indians irrigated a meager 1,500 acres. True, the Flathead received incidental benefits such as income from leasing, water-power development, and employment through the Civilian Conservation Corps–Indian Division. However, CCC-ID funds only went so far. In 1937-1938, work on project dams employed over two hundred Indians, but reductions in funding for 1939 cut that figure by fifty percent.[103]

Other unsettling problems resulted from CCC-ID work. The depression shut off "neighborhood employment"—such as cutting hay for non-Indians—and made surviving on subsistence gardens precarious, if not impossible. Commercial farming by Indians proved even more difficult. Thus, CCC-ID labor at Flathead, with its assured wages, inevitably pushed Indians away from the work the Indian Office saw as most proper, namely agriculture. The surety of income from non-farm employment opened new avenues for subsistence. While farming had been seasonal and irregular labor for many Indians, the CCC-ID and WPA "offered careers." What worried the BIA was that the New Deal would end and the battle to find jobs for Indians would begin anew. When the federal government cut appropriations for wage labor on irrigation works more problems ensued. Gordon MacGregor, of the Office of Indian Education, explained, "Little saving of wages had been made, and those who had farm lands had neither means nor equipment to put them into cultivation. In spite of the dire necessity to acquire some means of supporting themselves little disposition to return to farming has been shown by those able to do so." In fact, only about thirty-five percent took part in any sort of subsistence or commercial agriculture. Little wonder considering one-third of the Indian population owned no land, and another third had holdings "of impractical size" for profitable farming.[104]

On the Flathead Reservation, the process of allotment and irrigation revealed that views about, and use of, land and water were completely intertwined. Compensation remained a bone of contention. In 1922, the government appraised the value of reservoir sites at $40,000, in 1933 it offered the tribe $48,000—the appraisal plus four percent interest—and in 1935 the tribe rejected the offer. New appraisals in 1937 estimated the value at $159,311.95. The Flathead had lost a great deal to white settlers and the government, often without consideration for their wishes, and they did not intend to give up anymore. Three years later the Flathead Tribal Council passed a resolution opposing the sale of the reservoir sites and the passing of tribal title. The move forced the BIA to negotiate with the tribe and compensate them for the use of the sites with rental fees. Yet, by 1946, the government still had not paid the tribe.[105]

The only possible means of reparation lay with the U.S. Indian Claims Commission. Differing interpretations of the "value" of natural resources lay at the root of the Flathead case. Those values were as much cultural as economic. The value of water resources on the Flathead Reservation involved analysis of all tribal cessions of land to the government, going as far back as the treaty of 1855. Tribal attorneys contended that the government had always undervalued land on the reservation, compensating the tribe unfairly. For example, the streams and rivers on the lands ceded by the tribe in the nineteenth century flowed into the Columbia River Basin, and in western Montana, Oregon, and Washington irrigators diverted the water for agriculture. Thus, setting the value of water—and the remuneration

John Charley, successful Indian farmer, stacking hay, July 1914.
(NA 8NS-75-97-221, ARC293340)

to the tribe—might involve establishing its current worth. If runoff from treaty lands irrigated five million acres, and the current value of water per acre for irrigation was between fifty and seventy dollars in Montana and Washington, the government owed the Flathead tribe as much as one billion dollars.

E. O. Fuller, a consultant to tribal attorneys, claimed this argument had merit for a few key reasons. He explained, "The waters are a perpetual resource. They are not depleted. With each passing year the water is renewed…. Water is used, but due to constant renewal its value remains perpetually in the land." The question was not how did the tribe use its natural resources, but how had the resources been utilized after the tribe had ceded them at such an unjust price? More particularly, Fuller queried, "What have the…Treaty lands been worth to our government?" There was no clear-cut answer. However, definite information existed about numerous natural resources—water, timber, gold, silver, and other minerals—acquired by the government via the treaty. The total value of mineral production exceeded $2.5 billion and runoff water amounted to a similar figure. And, Fuller mused, what about the value of agricultural and livestock production that benefited from water on Stevens treaty lands in the last one hundred years? A cautious figure of three billion might serve as the price tag for all natural resources on lands ceded by the Flathead. However, the government only paid the tribe $360,000. Thus, the government and the public received more than $8,333 for each dollar paid the Indians—"a profit margin unheard of in commercial transactions." Was a crime committed, or had the government only put natural resources to use that the tribe would have never developed or utilized in the "best" and most "proper" manner? The injustice, Fuller concluded, was that "this transaction was conducted on behalf of the United States, by one who was charged with the duty of protecting" the Indian wards of the government.[106]

As for lands under the Flathead Irrigation Project, it did not matter whether the Indians used them the way the government or whites would. The significant point was that the land and water belonged to the tribe by treaty. If the government wanted those natural resources, then compensation for reservoir sites did not simply rest on the value of those lands for grazing and agriculture, but "in addition the highest value which the opportunity to use the sites" could potentially produce. The government envisioned reservoir sites, canals, and other project works in economic terms; land and water were property to be devoted to the "highest and best use." If federal officials applied those cultural values in order to appropriate resources, then the same standards had to be utilized when compensating the tribe. The Flathead deserved an amount equal to the "highest"—or most profitable— use of the land and water. Though many Flathead may not have seen dollar signs when they looked at their land, forests, and rivers, whites did. By applying the ideals of development, best use, and profit to expropriate natural resources, the federal government also set the measure for providing justice to the Indians. Like the tendrils of a watershed, economic returns from tribal rivers flowed along many different courses.[107]

Almost no fitting conclusion exists to the story of the Flathead Indians and the irrigation project. Construction began with bitter conflict that continued to the end. What started as an Indian project became a white project. By the end of World War II, the Indian Office had substantially completed construction. The story of irrigation at Flathead teaches many lessons. Historians have analyzed the Dawes Act of 1887 and allotment as a process of expropriation that created many of the social and economic problems on Indian reservations. Allotment at Flathead reveals the close ties between land and water. Water development and land dispossession went hand in hand. Moreover, the enterprise of irrigating Flathead relied on timber sales. In turn, white settlement relied on irrigation. Mixing those three—timbering, irrigating, and settling—proved complex. Many historians have written about Indians and water, but the story of forests, rivers and other natural resources is completely intertwined in Indian history. The complicated history of water utilization shows how making use of one component of nature vitally changed the meaning of the entire landscape. Above all, the Flathead Irrigation Project reveals the difficulty of reconciling Americans' divergent cultural conceptions of the environment.

Indians, non-Indians, and government officials often saw different things when they observed the Flathead environment. Carrying out the individual goals those different groups had for Indian natural resources meant inevitable conflict. The Indian Office lacked the ability to cooperate with other government agencies, as well as Indians and whites. In turn, conflicting visions for the future of the Flathead Valley created general discord between Indians and whites. Non-Indians and government officials—unlike many Indians—saw natural resources as something to be developed, put to "beneficial use," and profited from. That viewpoint enveloped and then transformed much of the Flatheads' historic beliefs about the environment. Attempts at making Indians "self-supporting"—of "civilizing the savage" and creating carbon copies of white, yeoman farmers—though not always successful, certainly changed Indian perspectives. Because the government reduced the environment to commodities, the Flathead eventually had to play the same game to gain justice. Indians did not wholly change, but continued to see their land, water, and other resources as the bedrock of tribal identity and strength. In the process, non-Indians—white settlers and government officials alike—were forced to concede part of their vision for an irrigated "agricultural empire." They had to accept its limitations and reconcile their own cultural values with the needs and desires of the Flathead Indians.

Standing oat crop of Michel Pablo, 1913.
(NA 8NS-75-97-221, box 7, F246)

# Chapter 2

# "A Lot of Trouble About Wood"

# Timber and Forestry on the Flathead Reservation

Tribal forests epitomized the interconnected nature of Indians' natural resources, as well as symbolized the contest between conservation and maximum use. And, like wildlife and water, people envisioned the woods on Indian lands through their cultural values. On the Flathead Reservation, timber represented the means to tribal subsistence and economic security. White lumber contractors often reaped rewards from Indian forests because of tribal needs for stable income. Alternately, the Indian Office confronted the conflicting demands for tribal subsistence through trees and national goals for the preservation of wilderness. Flathead forests served as a testing ground for Indian rights against broader American appeals for environmental protection. Managing nature meant controlling Indians.

By the last two decades of the nineteenth century, the Indian Office recognized that self-support for the Flathead Indians relied on their extensive natural resources. Though its primary policies focused on agriculture, the BIA realized that successful farming rested on utilizing tribal water and woods. Ironically, forests signified the advanced state of civilization among the Flathead compared to other tribes. Timber not only provided the means for constructing homes, barns, fences, churches, stores, and agency buildings, but the cash to purchase clothing, farming implements, seeds, and livestock. Achieving Indian acculturation into American society relied on the development of a tribal lumber industry. "Civilization" rushed onto the Flathead home in 1883 when the Northern Pacific Railroad entered the reservation on tracks laid with tribal timber. The construction of the Northern Pacific line across the southern end of the reservation was one of the most significant events in the nineteenth century at Flathead. The railroad brought white settlers, businessmen, and speculators, as well as new demands on the tribal landscape. The road ushered in a new era of economic expansion resting on increasing demands for lumber from Flathead forests.[1]

In the early years, putting timber to use was no easy feat. The government had "unfortunately located" the agency at the southern end of the reservation, making it difficult to transport trees to the sawmill. Most Indians lived in the Flathead Valley, more than twenty miles from the mill. Utilizing the "great abundancy of timber" relied on relocating the agency near Flathead Lake. As one Indian Office inspector paraphrased, "If resources [on the] reservation were developed, [the] Indians would be rich." The demands of the Northern Pacific furnished a good start. In return for the 2,734,000 feet of timber used for ties and trestles, the railroad "liberally" paid the tribe $5,458. In addition, the Indians received $7,626 for damages caused by the construction of the line. However, the company vacillated on settling the $16,000 debt it owed the Flathead for its right-of-way. Prior to 1883, the yearly production amounted to less than one hundred thousand feet. In that year, the figure rose to three hundred thousand, and in 1884 it jumped to five hundred thousand. In 1885, the railroad finally met all its obligations and the Indian agent distributed a per capita payment of over fourteen dollars to each Indian. Indeed, timber seemed to foreshadow a time when the Flathead would be "a very rich community."[2]

Not only wood, but water, drove the timber enterprise. In 1885, inspector Robert Gardner suggested using the waters of Mill Creek to power the agency saw and grist mills. Using the creek would save considerable expense, eliminating the need to pay an assistant miller and buy fuel and oil to run mill machinery. This economizing did not accurately reflect the profit flowing from lumbering near Flathead. The Interior Secretary reported that the Montana Improvement Company, of which the Northern Pacific owned fifty-one percent, had gotten more than its sanctioned share of wood from Flathead. The Interior Department permitted the erection of sawmills on tribal lands to supply wood for the railroad with the stipulation that the company would cease lumbering once the Northern Pacific had completed its line to Portland, Oregon. According to one report, however, when it finished the road, the company kept its mills "running night and day." "They have from two to three thousand men here steadily chopping the Government timber and sawing it up into lumber and shingles for their own benefit, and pocketing the proceeds themselves," reported S. H. Williams, a resident of Noxon, Montana, outside the reservation. "I don't think the law allows them to destroy the public timber as these men are doing." On December 4, 1885, Flathead Agent Peter Ronan, who fastidiously monitored lumbering operations by the company, emphatically denied that any timber theft occurred on the reservation. Thus, while allegations existed that the company cut lumber both on and outside tribal lands, it is only certain that illegal cutting happened off-reservation in direct defiance of government regulations.[3]

Timber trespass became so acute that the Interior Department ordered investigations into the dealings of the Northern Pacific, its subsidiaries, and other lumbering outfits. In 1887, the department radically increased the number of its special field agents for inspecting timber trespass and guarding public and Indian timber. The government filed suit against the Northern Pacific–Montana Improvement Company "timber syndicate" to recover $1.1 million in lost wood from 1883 to 1885.[4] The Montana Supreme Court decided against the United States, arguing that the western portion of the territory where the timber depredations occurred had not been surveyed by the General Land Office; without surveys verifying ownership and exact location, the court argued, the government could not prove that its property had been injured. The decision further "emboldened" the "marauders upon the public timber." Federal officials took custody of ties and other timber cut for the railroad. But, "in malign manner…terrorizing and overcoming" a U.S. Marshall and county sheriff, the company seized the wood and shipped it out of the territory. The illegal taking of timber, plus the large amount used for fences, mines, fuel, and that destroyed by fires, signaled an ever-increasing crisis. Montana Governor Preston Leslie concluded, "At the present rate of consumption and destruction our forests will soon disappear."[5]

The "rights" claimed by individual Americans to timber for personal use, development, and sale seemed to preclude any "duty" or obligation to protect public interests. The role of railroads and lumber companies in depleting forests and the consequent "wastefulness" transcended the boundaries of the West, inciting uproar across the nation. The great diminution, "if not exhaustion," as one Agriculture Department bulletin put it, demanded conservation. Because their future income relied on the timber supply, one official reasoned, it would seem that the railroads should "have a special interest in forest preservation." The department's fledgling forestry division, created in 1886, had a lot to learn about the dynamics of profit and loss in the lumber business. By the late 1880s, railroads were using the wood from 296,847 forested acres per year for maintenance and construction of track. The great abundance and cheapness of timber had made this possible, but now officials looked backward and wished that the land grant acts made to railroads had required them to ensure "a perpetual maintenance of a certain forest area to supply their future wants" through preservation or replanting.[6]

The lenience of federal forest policy taught important lessons. The "lavish liberality" represented the "pioneer experience," a time that was passing and had proven detrimental to the future of the West. Settlement and development, particularly in the Rocky Mountain West, required free access to timber. Unfortunately, the "need of home consumption" shared much less in "these spoils than the greed of lumbering monopolists." Forest officials admitted that the fault lay with the "charity" of federal laws, and now required new policies "in which the consumer pays for what he uses." Presaging Frederick Jackson Turner's theory about the closing of the frontier, the government recognized that natural resources required intelligent, "systematic management" as well as an ample dose of morality. These visionary proposals reflected a growing belief in the late-nineteenth century that forest protection interconnected with the maintenance of other resources. Preserving forests regulated water supply. Forestry division officials argued that in "forests the interlaced roots of the trees and the mass of leaves above act as a sponge, which absorbs the water and holds it long enough to enable it to perform its service of quickening animal and vegetable life." The water trickling through this sponge directly benefited regions immediate to forests by slowly nurturing streams and rivers and indirectly aided "distant localities" as water flowed through. Where streams were not protected "at their sources" in forests they could cause more injury than benefit through loss of water for crops and animals, as well as flood damage, soil erosion, and mudslides.[7]

These arguments about forest preservation directly connected with issues on tribal lands. The goals of the forestry division did not preclude timbering, only that forests should be "cultivated just like any other crop, and not wasted." The "most dense and continuous bodies of timber" lay along the western side of the Rocky Mountains, particularly in Montana, and their "careful conservation [was] of the greatest consequence." Proper use and protection of these "extensive and valuable" forests applied directly to the Flathead Reservation. In November 1888, the U.S. Attorney General emphasized this point by declaring that timber not needed for improvements, agriculture, or fuel by Indians was "the property of the United States." That rule, he proclaimed, would "doubtless preserve the timber on Indian reservations," and rather than wasting trees, tribal forests would "become a source of gain." Recognizing the extensive use and destruction of timber on non-Indian lands, or perhaps to make up for the loss of wood from the public domain, the Interior Department emphasized the preservation of Indian timber.[8]

Implementing these policies neglected cultural and climatic conditions. Prior to 1888, the Indian Office allowed Indians liberal cutting of timber for personal use and sale. The attorney general's 1888 decision, and a subsequent 1890 judgment, declared that wood "cut in trespass" on tribal land belonged to the government and not to tribes. As one BIA forest official later put it, these decisions were not based "on an enlightened consideration of existing economic conditions, a fitting apprehension of the moral rights of the Indians, and a due regard for the propriety of a generous guardianship over the wards of the nation." While the government could manage Indians, it proved impossible to control nature. In 1889-1890, lightning triggered major fires across western Montana and in the vicinity of Flathead Lake. The fires allegedly destroyed more timber "than could have been used by the entire population of the Territory in a generation." Smoke rolled across the reservation and "obscured the sun." The blazes consumed close to ninety thousand feet of timber and the loss neared $1.2 million. As the Interior Secretary summarized, "In consequence of the absence of a well-developed system of administration," the value of "forest property" continued to be "annually decimated" by fire and "illegal and wasteful cutting."[9]

Despite these problems, lumbering continued on the reservation. In the 1890s, small-scale sawmill operations supplied wood for constructing and shingling homes and other buildings for the Flathead. However, non-Indians continued to make inroads upon tribal forests. In 1894, the government filed suit against the Bitter Root Development Company for the illegal cutting of 31,525,000 feet of "saw logs" with a value over $315,000, but records only indicate that this occurred off-reservation on public lands near the reservation. Bitter Root Development, a subsidiary of the Anaconda Mining Company, supplied lumber for mines at Butte and Anaconda. In spite of orders to cease cutting, the company continued its timbering operations until 1897 with an average daily consumption of seven hundred cords and 100,000 feet of lumber.[10] Apparently, in an attempt to offset this consumption, the government made moves for forest preservation. On February 22, 1897, congress, impelled by Interior Department officials, created the Flathead and Lewis and Clarke Forest Reserves, setting aside over 4.2 million acres along the northern and eastern boundaries of the reservation. In addition, the Indian Office initiated negotiations for the cession of a forested mountain region on the west side of the reservation. The Indians refused to sell, and in 1901, after three years of failure, the BIA disbanded the negotiation commission.[11]

From 1899 to 1906, the federal government established another eight forest reserves in Montana, covering 4.7 million acres and bringing the total acreage to almost 9.4 million.[12] The creation of forest "reserves" belied the true nature of protection policies. In equal or greater proportion to preservation, the reserves provided new, but more regulated, business opportunities. In 1901, the Interior Department granted permits for three wagon roads, a boarding and lodging house, three hotels, three stores, a laundry, a livery and feed stable, a stage line, a steamboat, and six for hay cutting in the Flathead Forest Reserve. More importantly, the department promoted the reserves for cutting wood and pasturing livestock. For instance, in Lewis and Clarke and Flathead in 1903, ranchers grazed over 35,000 cattle and horses. In 1904, Interior sold over one million feet of timber and six thousand cords of wood from the two reserves.[13]

Though lumbering on the Flathead Reservation lagged in the early twentieth century, in 1906 it began a gradual ascent. Nature provided the impetus. In March of 1906, a severe windstorm swept across the reservation, uprooting close to eighteen million board feet of "merchantable green trees." The wood represented an economic windfall for the tribe. However, no federal law existed to authorize the sale of lumber on the reservation except for dead timber. While it awaited presidential consent for selling the trees, the Indian Office asked Agent Samuel Bellew to take bids for the sale of the wood. Proposals ranged from twenty-five cents to $1.25 per MBM (1,000 feet). The BIA rejected the offers as grossly "inadequate," and requested that the Agriculture Department detail a forest division employee to inspect and appraise the timber. Chief Forester Gifford Pinchot sent inspector A. K. Chittenden, who, to the consternation of the Indian Office, agreed with the value of $1 to $1.25. In August, President Theodore Roosevelt authorized the sale, and the BIA instructed Bellew to advertise in regional newspapers. The BIA granted a contract to the Ed Donlan and W. B. Rusell outfit and the O'Brien Lumber Company. In total, the two companies cut twenty-three million feet of lumber, bringing in $29,000 in net proceeds.[14]

With the upsurge of lumbering at Flathead, the BIA discovered that it needed to put forestry on a more systematized basis. The opening of the reservation to white settlement required the classification of tribal lands. In 1907, it sent the "Salzman Commission," headed by Interior Forest Service employee F. X. Salzman, to establish land values. The commission included two other government men and two Indians, John Matt and Angus McDonald. To protect Flathead interests, the lands had to be designated in one of four classes: agricultural, timber, mineral, or grazing. In 1908, to ensure that the tribe would gain appropriate compensation from its timber, the Secretaries of Interior and Agriculture entered into a cooperative agreement for managing forests in a manner "just to the Indians." The two agencies wanted to determine "the best permanent use" of Flathead lands. With the forests, they intended to "apply management plans; to sell such timber as may be cut without injury to the forest; to supervise the logging under methods which will improve the forest and yield the full market value of all the timber cut; and to protect all forests on Indian reservations whether they are being cut over or not." This mix of preservation and use indicated the growing national push for the conservation of natural resources.[15]

However, Flathead forests could be utilized for many enterprises. Montana Senator Joseph M. Dixon insisted that the Reclamation Service supervise timber sales because properly funding the "great irrigation enterprise" of the Flathead Project relied on those funds. The 1908 proposal planned to market tribal forests for fifteen years, enabling sufficient sales to fund reclamation. The BIA intended to sell all land left after timber removal with the income going to the benefit of the tribe. By separating the sale of timber and disposal of land, the government hoped to prevent forest fires; if speculators bought land and timber together they might remove the marketable wood and leave ignition-prone brush behind. In short, the quickest profit came from the timber, rather than the land itself, and by separating the sales, the Indian Office—and thus the Flathead tribe—could reap the most benefit.[16]

The negotiations for managing Flathead timber occurred within the midst of a larger national push for forest conservation. In 1908, President Roosevelt established a "National Conservation Commission" composed of state governors. Protection of natural resources had become the "most weighty question" facing the United States. As Thomas Will, secretary of the American Forestry Association, explained, "Many of these resources, together with interests and problems directly involved—inland navigation, power, floods, irrigation, drainage, soil conservation and the public health—constitute an arch of which the forest is keystone." Because the "proper care of the forest resources of the country [was] a State as well as National problem," Roosevelt instructed the governors to create state conservation committees to supplement the federal efforts. Forests seemed to be disappearing at such a rate as to threaten exhaustion, and provoked fears that the "shadow of a timber famine" was "upon the land." The states and the nation had to protect against timber theft and fires, combining their efforts to promote wise use and the renewal of forest resources. In turn, this required cooperation by the various federal agencies present on tribal lands. This meant systematizing and putting into action the theories of late-nineteenth century forest advocates. The "most important subject" was the "relation of forests to water supply in all its phases." Thus, the addition of the Reclamation Service to the Indian Office and Forest Service created the trinity of conservation on Indian lands.[17]

In 1908, the connection between timbering and irrigation began to increase. The Flathead Irrigation Project engineer began requesting large amounts of wood to build flumes, headgates, dams, and other project structures. Agent Samuel Bellew set up a mill in the Jocko River Valley and Indians began hauling timber and sawing it for use by the Reclamation Service. A congressional act on March 3, 1909, provided for the sale of timber and agricultural land and supplemented the original act for allotment at Flathead. By late 1909, $300,000 had been raised from the sale of timber to outside contractors and the disposal of a small portion of surplus tribal lands. But not all seemed to be working out as planned. In what turned out to be a huge understatement, Senator Dixon reported to Reclamation Director Frederick H. Newell and Interior Secretary Richard A. Ballinger, "I understand there is liable to be some possible division of opinion regarding the handling of the timber on the Flathead Reservation."[18]

Though rumblings of discontent existed from the beginning, the first signs of serious "division" began to appear in early January of 1909. The primary problem stemmed from the competing aims of different federal agencies. Power disputes between Interior Secretary Ballinger and Chief Forester Gifford Pinchot erupted over the ultimate desired extent of forest preservation. Pinchot certainly supported wise-use, but Ballinger apparently believed that concessions should be made to private corporations. Some newspapers went so far as to accuse the secretary of being swayed by "special and powerful interests" who were "active in seizing the forest and water power resources." Some said the disagreement spilled over into a more widespread battle between the "common folk" and the "trusts." They contended that westerners supported the regulation of railroads and other corporations but had contempt for "government interference" in individual rights to natural resources. This, the *New York Post* argued, was what westerners termed "Pinchotism," complaining that government regulation inhibited "their putting the axe to the tree as freely as their fathers did."[19]

In the summer of 1909, the contest reached a head. Ballinger increasingly took offense to the role of Agricultural Secretary Horace Wilson and the recommendations of Pinchot. Thus, only fifteen months after consummating the agreement, Interior disbanded cooperation between the Indian Office and the Forest Service. Ballinger claimed he terminated collaboration because of the limitations of "divided responsibility" and differences of opinion on laws regulating natural resources. Disagreements over timber directly related to water resources. Ballinger, via allotment, purportedly opened lands to settlement on Indian reservations set aside by Pinchot for water and power sites as well as timber protection. Administrative accountability was an important issue and Ballinger believed that the Reclamation Service was not telling the truth about its projects. He directed his ire at Reclamation Director Newell for applying unsound "business methods" to irrigation development. At the root of both quarrels were divergent views about the best methods for disposing of the public domain and Indian lands that contained valuable natural resources. Pinchot defended a stronger federal presence, believing in the "intrinsic wisdom of trained government bureaucrats in making management decisions." Ballinger, it seemed, supported increased "private activity" in resource development. Despite the "absence of men" in the Indian Office "technically qualified" for carrying out timber protection, Pinchot complained that Ballinger emphasized BIA authority and obstructed the advisory role of the Forest Service when managing Indian timber.[20]

The Ballinger-Pinchot affair was a complex battle over national interests.[21] Although Pinchot, Newell, and many others accused Ballinger of pandering to corporate interests, in his annual reports he claimed to want nothing more than to eliminate American destruction of the public domain. Ballinger asserted, "It is to be regretted that we, as a nation, were so tardy to realize the importance of preventing so large a measure of our natural resources passing into the hands of land pirates and speculators, with no view to development looking to the national welfare." Development remained the "keynote" in conservation, yet he stressed "safeguarding" the disposition of natural resources in the interest of the "public good as against private greed." Between 1860 and 1910, the public domain had declined from over one billion acres to less than 730 million plus lands within Indian reservations. Ballinger implied that tribal lands represented some of the best places left for conserving resources. Yet Pinchot cited "improper logging rules" for selling two million feet of Flathead timber as a key example of BIA mismanagement under Ballinger's reign. To ensure against continuing along an "unlawful" and "wasteful course" in regard to timber, congress appropriated $100,000 for forestry work in "Indian country." In late 1909, the BIA began to develop its forestry division to "comprehensively administer" tribal timber "property."[22]

When a meteorite crashed into a mountainous, timbered region on the western boundary of the Flathead Reservation in May 1910, it seemed to augur a new course in Indian forest management. Increasingly, the Indian Office emphasized that Flathead timber was an "asset" for the benefit of the tribe, rather than non-Indians.[23] Superintendent Fred C. Morgan estimated that 1.8 billion feet of yellow pine, red fir, spruce, cedar, and lodgepole pine existed on Flathead. In heavily wooded areas, there was as much as twenty-five thousand feet of timber per acre. Sawed boards went for seventeen dollars per one thousand feet and between $3.25 and $4 per cord. Morgan emphasized the removal and sale of mature timber to make way for younger growth. Clearing dead wood would retard the spread of forest fires, provide space for fighting fires, and "given proper care and protection," allow for the reforestation of bare areas. Indians used wood for the "greater part" in making improvements to their allotments. Discouraged by this, Morgan complained, "The Indians of this reservation seem to take little interest in the timber resources, probably because they do not fully realize the value of the timber, not only its value for lumber, but its value for the conserving of the water supply." Putting timber "on the market as rapidly as possible" would foster conservation and provide income, whether the Indians wanted it or not.[24]

In 1910, perhaps the most disastrous forest fire in U.S. history struck Idaho and Montana. The "Big Fire" ravaged three million acres, burning eight billion feet of timber.[25] The government planned to salvage as much of the charred timber as possible. Undoubtedly a praiseworthy effort, but it did not bode well for Indians. Making use of the burnt-over forests was "a wise step toward the better conservation of the public resources." However, the glutted market would not support the production of other timber. The Indian Office offered sixty million feet of Flathead timber for sale and received no bids. Thus, under orders from Secretary Ballinger, the tribe sacrificed several years of timber production. The situation meant the loss of per capita payments and the delay of irrigation construction. However, the tribe received indirect benefits. Every available man—Indians, non-Indians, and agency employees—spent the greater part of July and August fighting fires on and near the reservation. Superintendent Morgan spent $11,558 for suppression, part of which went to pay the Flathead for their labor.[26]

To his dismay, Morgan learned that in addition to problems with timber management, he faced increasing obstacles from non-Indians. After the government opened the Flathead Reservation to white settlement in 1910, it immediately received over eighty thousand applications for land. Despite its aims for the judicious administration of the Indian landscape, the BIA quickly learned that opposing speculation was easier than stopping it. *The Ronan Pioneer*, the mouthpiece for white residents, encouraged white settlement in a manner that contributed to conflict. Its "great scheme" for homesteading and letting the "timber go with the land" emphasized agricultural use over forestry. In turn, its plan to educate the "department at Washington along proper lines" stressed that the desires of settlers should take precedence over and would benefit the nation more than the needs and interests of the Flathead.[27]

As a result of the *Pioneer's* efforts, the General Land Office faced a wave of squatters and speculators who flooded onto tracts classified as timberland and believed they could capitalize on the easy profit promised by the newspaper. While the government criticized the greed of whites, the *Pioneer* accused the Land Office of conspiring against innocent settlers.

The *Pioneer* believed that the government meant to give the land to a "big company or coterie of favored friends," arguing the plot "was the big colored person in the reservation woodpile." Whether or not the newspaper was correct, the Indian Office reported that the opening of the reservation led to a condition "conducive to timber trespass." In one critical case, the BIA revealed it had failed to prevent the Polson Lumber Company from illegally cutting 600,000 feet of logs from Indian allotments. Ironically, settlers and federal officials disregarded their common aim: regardless of the economic or conservation value of trees, both intended to remove them because they saw agriculture as more beneficial.[28]

The problems with settlers revealed federal officials' inability to work with outside interests. In 1911, an appraisal commission was authorized to reevaluate lands at Flathead, and when they conducted the appraisal they found that many tracts were more valuable for timber than agriculture or grazing. Though this closed the lands to homesteaders, poor communication between the Indian and General Land Offices led to the approval of many filings. Believing that the Indian Office had no authority in the matter, whites proceeded to sell timber on land they settled. Fearing that "hundreds of 'squatters'" and speculators would steal Indian—or government—land, the Indian Office subjectively chose a date when it believed it had informed the Land Office about the classification of timberlands. Because of the Land Office mistake and the "apparent good faith of some of these squatters," the BIA confirmed the entries for those who filed prior to the date. Those filing afterward had their claims rejected, and the Indian Office insisted on "forcible dispossession." Many settlers protested that either the Land Office misinformed them, or that the appraisal commission overestimated the amount of timber and "erroneously classified" the tracts.[29]

The *Ronan Pioneer* continued its "organized attempt to create public sentiment sufficient to force" settlement of timbered lands, arguing the wood had little value and "praising the quality of the land" for farming. However, federal appraisals fixed the value of Flathead timber at over $4.5 million. By 1912, settlers proclaimed that Interior Department "red tape and dilatory tactics" retarded development, bringing "shame" to what could easily have been "a beautiful and productive country." The criticism seemed duplicitous in light of *Pioneer* advertising that proclaimed, "We Have Lumber.... Remember this is RESERVATION PINE; it looks like beauty and lasts for ages." In fact, the Indian Office did not oppose "improvement of the country" so long as it was directed towards its goals for the reservation. Congress appropriated $20,000 for an agency sawmill. In the first half of 1912, the Reclamation and Indian Bureaus sawed and sold nearly 1.5 million feet of lumber to reimburse funding for the irrigation project. This trend foreshadowed a rapid growth in lumbering on the Flathead Reservation.[30]

The increasing development of timber promised progress toward achieving the goals of federal policy on Indian natural resources. It represented government officials' vision of themselves as the "guardian of this vast Indian estate." In 1913, Commissioner Cato Sells reflected, "How this property shall be conserved for the benefit of the Indians and how they shall be taught to make the best possible use thereof so that they may ultimately take their rightful place as self-supporting citizens of the Republic are the great problems confronting this bureau." The close relationship between natural resources remained central to government policy. The government managed tribal timber, Sells maintained, to "derive a sustained revenue adequate to provide for the needs of the Indians as agricultural development takes place within the Indian reservations and yet not affect unfavorably the future needs both as regard the timber and water supply." Indians' "valuable timber" represented a "very potent agency in promoting their progress." Sells concluded that the "solution to the [Indian] problem" required "sound business foresight, enlightened by the scientific principles…of both forestry and irrigation." His aims were laudable, even if he emphasized federal visions over Indian beliefs about nature.[31]

In spite of the problems posed by the fire of 1910, the BIA placed increasing emphasis on timbering. In 1913, the Flathead, contractors, and federal employees cut close to 4.2 million feet. The timber removed by Indians and the government was used to construct irrigation works and buildings for the agency and individual Indians. Moreover, outside contractors took close to three million feet of lumber for sale throughout Montana and across the West. Production in the first half of 1914 was much the same. The value of timber cut by all parties amounted to about $30,000. It is unclear what the tribe received besides the benefit of improvements. However, contractors clearly paid a stumpage fee to the Indian Office well below what they sold lumber for.[32] The BIA also developed a system for the protection of timber, employing ten Indian and white forest guards. This move hinted at the serious concerns about timber trespass and forest fires. While lumbering had by no means made the Flathead self-supporting, the industry at least provided decent homes and farm buildings for a good portion of the tribe.[33]

By 1914, land disputes reached critical levels. Non-Indians continued to squat on timberland that they desired to clear for farms, and to settle lands within waterpower and reservoir sites or lands reserved for Indian allotments, despite the rejection of their entries. In turn, needing money for subsistence, many Flathead began getting their allotments patented and selling the land. These land transfers frequently occurred through deceptive means. BIA officials questioned the "competency" of the Flathead to judiciously manage their land. White land speculators, often working for outside investors living on the East coast, "secured a good deal of business" by convincing them of the immediate rewards of selling their patent rights. By expediting the issuance of patents and influencing Indians, speculators gained advance notice of land sales. That knowledge provided "opportunity for land sharks and creditors to line up their affairs so as to pounce on the Indian at once and arrange a contract for immediate sale at private price."[34]

Timbering and allotment went hand-in-hand. Superintendent Fred Morgan informed the Indian Office that, as a result of easy access to allotments, nearly three times as much timber had been cut on individual lands as on communal tribal lands. Yet white homesteaders increasingly bought wood from tribal lands "in the hope of securing a filing on such land after the cutting and removal of the timber." In 1914, the BIA sent William Ketcham to investigate the predicament. A 1913 appraisal of the lands revealed divergent values from those made by the Salzman Commission in 1908, more than tripling their worth. Settlers that made entry and improvements six years prior, in the expectation of cheap land, now faced a purchase price beyond their means. The Indians had a right to the higher price, while settlers had an equal claim to the initial cost. Ketcham also indicated that reservation settlement portended a time when whites would own the majority of Flathead lands, the Indians would be unable to support themselves, and as a result, the government might be forced to purchase lands for "homeless Flathead Indians." He concluded that the timberlands, "if properly conserved and utilized," offered a partial answer. The solution was not in forest conservation, but in the removal and sale of trees to make way for pastures for Indian stockmen. Ketcham looked toward Indians' best interests, but he saw their survival in cheaply "disposing of the timber" as rapidly as possible.[35]

Ketcham interviewed a number of white claimants to land entries on the reservation. He reported that many "applied for timbered lands as a last resort" and not merely because they wanted to "remove stumps." Rather, most had similar intentions to William Howe who was "hard-working," merely "came west to better himself," and had been "sorely disappointed" with the settlement conditions. Howe's brother Chester complained that his entry had been rejected because it had been classified as timbered land, even though the tract contained more stones than trees. He stated that the timber requirements were a "drawback and discouragement" to development, requesting reconsideration of his land application so he could begin "homesteading with a happy heart." By late 1914, more than two hundred cases existed on the reservation where non-Indians had filed on tracts classified as timberlands, and all claimed that that their selections were more valuable for agriculture than lumber. Nevertheless, in many cases, the government refused to give the same lands to Indians as allotments based on the claim that the timber would produce more value than farming.[36]

Assessing the land based on the value of trees or farm production proved an intricate process. The actions of both non-Indians and federal officials complicated the affair. Despite the claims of white settlers to the contrary, timber had great worth even if a tract only contained a small stand. Though saw lumber generally went for two to three dollars per one thousand feet, the demand for land drove up the price for timber on the reservation. Some of the most valuable land for agriculture and horticulture lay along Flathead Lake and twenty miles southward to Mission Creek, and trees covered the area. The fact that the land in that area needed very little irrigation made it all the more precious. Provisions in the act opening the reservation to settlement required the removal of trees prior to the acceptance of homestead entries. Thus, the Indian Office made contracts with "quite a number of people" to purchase the timber and then to cut and sell it. In short, they were cutting down forests just to have farmland. However, the BIA was "so very anxious to help there [sic] dependent Indians and make a good annual report of their stewardship," as the *Ronan Pioneer* put it, that the Indian Office made "extortionate appraisals of the timbers." Superintendent Morgan let lumber contracts to settlers for four to five dollars per thousand feet, and required timber removal within one year. If white farmers demanded access to valuable agricultural lands, then the Indian Office—and the Flathead tribe—would capitalize on the sale of trees.[37]

Supply and demand was the name of the game and the Indian Office dealt the deck. The BIA intended to both take profit and promote pleasure from the timbered lands at Flathead. In the summer of 1915, it put 889 parcels of land along Flathead Lake up for sale. Though timber did not entirely cover all of these plots, most contained trees. These two- to five-acre "Flathead villa sites" offered Americans the chance for scenic getaways. The sites, having an appraised value of $35,000, sold for a whopping sum of $125,000 and some went for as much as $300 an acre. The revenue went to the credit of the tribe. Apparently, farming and timbering were not the only ways to make Indian land productive.[38]

The Flathead lumber industry began to boom in 1916. Superintendent Morgan reported a sixty percent increase in timber sales over the previous year. Besides the sale of timber to hopeful homesteaders, more important developments contributed to the dramatic upsurge. As Indian Commissioner

Cato Sells explained, the appropriation act of 1916 contained provisions aimed at "bringing into productive use" tracts classified as timberlands and that could not be homesteaded until the "timber was disposed of." Most of these lands lay along the base of the Mission Range and in the vicinity of the town of Ronan. Fortunately, the Northern Pacific Railroad decided to construct a branch line between Dixon on the south to Polson on the north—passing directly through Ronan. The stands of timber were "so heavy that homesteaders could not conveniently pay the full value of the timber." But the rail line made it possible to transport huge amounts of lumber, making the timber more marketable. The BIA decided that putting the land to productive use—agriculture—necessitated the sale of huge amounts of wood. The railroad "made accessible some of the best timber on agricultural lands" and the Indian Office offered sixty million feet of wood for sale. Reservation officials rejoiced that in the coming year it was probable that timber operations would increase two hundred percent.[39]

World War I increased the demand for timber, and the reservation lumber industry flourished. The declaration of war against Germany on April 6, 1917, Sells argued, required "a special effort...to place upon the market timber suitable for war purposes and to encourage in every practical way the production of those timber products that would be of special advantage in supplying the military and industrial needs incident to the war." Though Flathead lumber did not go directly into war uses, Sells continued, it "will supply needs that arise through the diversion of other timber products to military purposes." In the first half of 1917, the Flathead timber business increased one hundred percent over the previous year. Sales reached 125 million feet from lands destined for homesteading by white farmers.[40]

The rate of cutting seemed a recipe for extensive deforestation. J. P. Kinney, Chief Forester for the Indian Office, and Superintendent Sharp collaborated to sell all available wood on lands desired for agriculture. In the spring of 1917, the Polleys Lumber Company won a bid for forty-seven million board feet at a price of $160,000. The BIA awarded the Heron Lumber Company a contract for sixty-two million feet for $228,000. The revenue to the tribe generally covered expenses for household and farming equipment, clothing, and "general support." Money from timber became the mainstay for tribal subsistence. The situation prompted Superintendent Sharp to worry, "The reasoning of the Indians seems to be, 'Why work when there is money in the bank not yet spent?' and they are persistent and aggressive in their demands for money." Self-support seemed to take on new meanings when it involved the lumber industry. Though he meant it in derision, Sharp was right about Flathead demands for "pocket money" from timber sales. When asked why they wanted money from tribal funds,

Indians' "usual answer" was "It is my money, not your money, not [the] Government's money."[41]

Despite the flush economic conditions during the "great war," signs of danger began to appear. Looking back on the situation, J. P. Kinney concluded that "land hungry adventurers" surged "about the borders of Indian reservations, whetting their land appetites on various morsels of misinformation with respect to the fortunes lying dormant...within the illogical and arbitrary boundaries of Indian reservations." Their "misdirected enthusiasm" portended a time when "abandoned shacks" would litter the Flathead Reservation. What Kinney failed to mention was that the government encouraged these homesteaders. From 1917 to 1918, the Indian and General Land Offices opened more than 2,600 acres of "nontimbered" and over 10,000 acres of timberland. In the latter case, the land appraised for $46,000 and the timber for close to $81,000. Rules required payment for one-third of the price of the land and the entire value of the timber at the time of entry. In pursuit of a homestead, many settlers mortgaged themselves to the hilt. In 1918, ten sawmills operated on the reservation, cutting timber valued at $175,000 for Indians, the government, and contractors. The pursuit of profit seemed to override rationality.[42]

In 1919, the tribal timber industry continued to surge. Sales brought in $188,000. Six new sawmills went up on the reservation to manage the increased output. However, the profits did not provide contentment. Angered by federal management of their land and resources, the Flathead held a mass meeting and drew up a petition for self-government. They believed that tribal timberlands sold by the government had a value closer to several million dollars than the $100,000 that came to the reservation. The Flathead only received $40,000 of that sum; the rest went to pay agency officials and "general management" purposes.[43]

In 1919, House hearings indicated that when the Indian Office disbanded its cooperative work with the U.S. Forest Service in 1909, greater tumult existed than was revealed at the time. Divided responsibility—the Forest Service having authority in the field and the BIA assuming responsibility for funding—led to conflicts of interest. The service concentrated on "scientific forestry," while the Indian Office focused on the "welfare and advancement of the Indians who owned the forest property." The "divorcement of authority" contributed to friction and "misunderstandings" about the purpose of administering Indian forests. Yet between 1909 and 1919, it certainly seemed that BIA control of forestry had not lived up to its purported dedication to the "welfare" of the Indians. Or, perhaps federal officials felt they had. But as the Flathead mass meeting indicated, the Indians believed the Indian Office failed to consider their wishes.[44]

As Indian lumbering continued to boom in the early 1920s, conservationists began to intercede. In 1920, Flathead timber sales generated $221,000. The following year seventeen private sawmills operated on the reservation, cutting nearly 52,000,000 feet of timber valued at $215,000. In turn, an increasing number of fires wreaked havoc on a large amount of merchantable timber. The Indian Office reasoned it was high time to apply more "prudent administration" to Flathead forests. It based regulations on wise-use and its vision of the best interests of the tribe. Federal Indian forest policy focused on providing an abundant supply of timber to Indians for fuel, utilizing mature timber for home and farm construction, and sale to lumber contractors. The BIA also pointed to a higher goal for lumbering: "to give younger growth an opportunity for development" and guarantee a future supply of fuel for Indians.[45]

Conservation of timber not only proved integral to protecting Indian rights, but to the Flathead Irrigation Project. When a forest official proposed the sale of twenty-one million feet of timber near Dog Lake, non-Indians protested and instead proposed a public park. The Indian Office vetoed the request, arguing the Reclamation Service had reserved the land. Still, Commissioner Sells echoed the non-Indian residents' plea by recommending the sale of timber with an eye to "the reservation of timber about the lake as will insure the preservation of the scenic qualities of the locality." As with allotment, timbering and irrigating were mutual enterprises. Lumbering camps and the Reclamation Service offered the Flathead "plenty of employment," and firefighting provided summer work. Via reclamation, timber benefited the white residents of the reservation almost as much as the tribe. In 1920, under advice from the House and Senate Committees on Indian Affairs, Interior Secretary Franklin K. Lane instituted a commission to investigate and implement forest preservation. The commission—including members of the Indian Office, Reclamation Service, and U.S. Forest Service—wanted to conserve timber to protect watersheds, the flow of streams being vital for irrigation. Recall that by the 1920s, the irrigation project was providing more benefits for white settlers than Indians.[46]

Congress, backed by the Indian forest commission's report, offered other important reasons for timber preservation. Drought contributed to fires that "taxed to the utmost the facilities of the [Indian] Service for the protection of forests." The BIA began taking decisive steps to improving telephone communication systems with a "view to increasing the efficiency of the fire control plans." Legislation sought by Secretary Lane proposed the establishment of a national forest out of Flathead timberlands not already allotted or reserved.[47] Federal officials believed that making the lands into a national forest would afford more "proper supervision" of cutting, watershed preservation, and that Indian property adjacent to the forest would be "more amply protected from destruction by fire" because the U.S. Forest Service was "better equipped for such purpose."[48]

Conservation—wise-use—of forests created great benefits for the tribe. Timber sales produced direct subsistence income as well as funds to establish enterprises of "incalculable value to the advancement of the Indians industrially, socially, and morally." For instance, funds from timber sales at Flathead fostered beadwork and other native industries, as well as money for home and farm improvements, livestock, and consumer goods. As Superintendent Charles E. Coe simply summarized, "The greatest asset of the Flathead Indians is in the timber." Coe alternately argued that the moralizing and civilizing aspects of timbering income did not always live up to expectations. Many Indians preferred to rely on the considerable per capita payments for subsistence rather than "make the effort to farm."[49]

Extensive lumbering had pros and cons. In 1922, contractors cut 2.8 million board feet and the BIA contracted out an additional 135 million feet. In the early 1920s, fires ravaged an annual average of seven thousand acres on the reservation and the agency spent over $10,000 a year for firefighting. Drought and poor cutting practices played a large role. Lumbering produced huge amounts of slash; it left debris strewn across cutover areas and provided perfect tinder. The problem of contractors failing to dispose of slash had grown to such an extent that Superintendent Coe served written notice on the large operators stating the BIA would cancel their cutting contracts if they did not immediately clean up their mess. Moreover, extensive sawing at mills offered the perfect fuel for fire. In 1923, two white contractors sued the Northern Pacific for a blaze that destroyed their lumberyard. Railroad employees carelessly let oil accumulate by tracks near the yard. Engineer Matt Jahr failed to properly maintain his locomotive and the engine threw sparks onto the oil and the fire then leapt into the sawmill. The lumbermen sued for $236,766 in lost machinery, buildings, timber, and future contracts they could not fulfill.[50]

Nevertheless, the Flathead lumber industry continued to flourish. In one month in 1923, contractors cut close to 4.2 million feet of timber. The Interior Department made a "special effort" to promote and "draw attention to the opportunities" of lumbering in Indian forests. That year logging on all Indian reservations brought in over seven million dollars. The value of timber cut at Flathead in 1923 and 1924 amounted to almost one half million dollars. Lumbering profits exceeded the expectations of federal officials. Flathead timbering had become a big business.[51]

The 1924 cut produced the largest output ever at Flathead, and it raised concerns. By 1925, the demand for conservation grew so great that

President Calvin Coolidge declared a "National Forest Week." He called for a change in the "national attitude" toward forests, declaring, "We have too freely spent the rich and magnificent gift that nature bestowed on us. In our eagerness to use that gift we have stripped our forests." Coolidge emphasized conservation, replanting, and reforestation. Americans needed "to treat [their] forests as crops, to be used, but also to be renewed." He proclaimed they had a "sacred responsibility" to future generations, and unless they used the "gifts of Divine Providence" with gratitude and restraint, they would prove themselves "unworthy guardians of a heritage... held in trust" for all.[52]

The Interior Department and its sub-agencies heeded Coolidge's appeal. As during the Roosevelt administration, it seemed that the country faced a "timber famine." Indian lumber was no exception. In fact, forests on tribal lands increasingly represented an ecological safety-net for American natural resources. The problem was most critical on fee patent allotments, where ownership had passed from federal to individual control on the "assumption" that allottees "were competent" and had frequently been sold for a fraction of its value. The Indian Forestry Service applied "conservative management" to tribal lands, but timbered allotments required a "decidedly different policy." The dilemma was that the primary purpose of allotment focused on providing "a home for the Indian," and it proved difficult to apply forest regulations "ideally suited" for tribal lands to small tracts of forty to one hundred acres. On reservations like Flathead, much of the land contained timber, and thus forested land had to "be allotted if allotments were to be made." Because much of the property also had agricultural value, some Flathead and the Indian Office desired clear cutting. Even when allotments were "poorly adapted to agricultural use," removing the trees seemed vital for subsistence. The BIA finally had to confront the contradictions between its policy goals for making Indians into yeoman farmers and utilizing forests.[53]

Indian Office administrators viewed the forestry dilemma in different ways. In 1926, the Commissioner of Indian Affairs concluded that the ten-year period between 1917 and 1926 represented an unequaled success in the opportunities reaped from timbering on tribal lands.[54] However, J. P. Kinney, the director of Indian Forestry, saw the results in another light. Though the BIA had considered it best to clear-cut timber from allotments to make way for agriculture, Kinney now doubted the advisability of that policy. By 1927, the decline of wheat and other crop prices since World War I had caused an "almost complete cessation" of land development for farming, and after removing the trees, many of the farms had been abandoned. Since 1920, no serious demand had existed from whites for

homesteads within reservations, but the "attractive prices" of timber from
tribal lands "thoroughly aroused the acquisitive instincts of individual
Indians." The need of funds for individual assistance and for the support
of tribal enterprises necessitated the sale of large quantities of timber but
was not made on a "theoretically sound basis from a forestry viewpoint."
The conditions injected "an element of uncertainty" into Indian forestry
"that can hardly fail to shake the resolution of any forester" who believed
in preservation and reforestation, Kinney concluded. As much as Kinney
deplored "such improper and uneconomic use of forest land," there seemed
no other possible course.[55]

During the rest of the 1920s, federal officials complained that an
"unfavorable lumber market" affected production at Flathead. They were
only partly correct. Oversupply did lead to slightly lower prices, dropping
about seventy cents per thousand feet. However, the volume of trade
maintained high levels through the first half of 1930. Then, like all American
economic endeavors, the Great Depression struck Flathead timbering. From
1929 to 1930, the volume cut dropped from sixty-three million feet to forty-
nine million. Then the bottom dropped out. In 1931, the amount declined to
ten million, and by 1933 to a mere 800,000. The Flathead timber industry
would not again reach the mid-1920s level of success until the 1960s.[56]

As timbering declined, the Interior Department began to consolidate
natural resource work. The Secretary ordered the BIA's forestry branch
to take over the supervision of grazing activities. Ironically, the Indian
Commissioner admitted that the task would be difficult considering the
cooperation it required—the BIA had consistently shown that teamwork
was not its strong suit. However, the demands of conservation made grazing
and forestry a likely pairing because both contributed to soil erosion and
watershed damage. Protecting Indian forest and range promised to align all
BIA conservation goals.[57]

Moreover, Flathead forests offered prime grazing. Before 1920, the
"Indians were not in sympathy with the grazing of sheep on timber lands,"
purportedly going so far as setting fire to the timber to get rid of the animals.
But once the tribe began to receive economic returns from grazing their
attitudes changed. By the early 1930s, Flathead forests harbored nearly
thirty thousand sheep. Yet, as Flathead Reservation forest supervisor
Charles Faunce indicated, conservation was the key purpose for grazing
timberlands. Grazing protected timber because the sheep rid the forest
floor of flammable brush and grasses. In fact, one employee reported, the
most serious fires in recent years had occurred on lands not being grazed
regularly. Proper grazing practices did not prevent the development of a
"timber crop" nor did it hamper reforestation. Forest fire protection also

meant sustaining watersheds and potential for recreation. Though sheep often ate ravenously, controlling their numbers left enough feed for wildlife. Finally, and perhaps taking the argument a bit far, Faunce contended that this type of forest protection preserved birds and fish because it ensured stream flow by maintaining proper ground cover and extinguishing fires.[58]

As the depression destroyed the lumber industry at Flathead, drought contributed to the decimation of forests. Though worse on the Great Plains, between 1928 and 1931 Montana and the Northwest received less than half its normal precipitation. In 1931, severe electrical storms accompanied the extreme drought, sparking small fires that hot, dry winds fanned into enormous conflagrations. The lack of roads and trails into forested areas at Flathead limited the mobility of fire equipment and frequently prevented crews from reaching "incipient fires." Thus, suppression required larger crews working for longer periods and at greatly increased costs. The reservation lost an enormous $50,000 worth of timber and the cost of control reached $100,000. With depressed markets and ravenous fires, forests seemed to be more of a disadvantage than an asset. When John Collier became Commissioner of Indian Affairs, he intended to change that.[59]

In 1933, Collier outlined his plans for Indian natural resources. "We must…impose on the Indian forests, by congressional enactment, the principle that only the forest income may be used and the forest capital must be left unimpaired," he noted. "This principle may one day become a guide to point the way to saving the forests of America." The problems of Indian forestry, Collier argued, grew out of allotment and a "*laissez-faire* economic philosophy that has ridden our land wellnigh to ruin." He saw the failures of forestry as developing from the conflict between preservation and profit, or the desire to have "just as good trees fifty years from now" and immediate economic returns. Allotment resulted in the division of Indian forests into 160-acre individual units. Divided ownership meant different opinions about management and rendered sustained-yield policies futile. Collier lamented, "the only rational course was to sell the Indian timber to the highest bidder, practice such forestry as the allottees or buyers would tolerate, and get as much money as possible." This, he argued, had many deleterious effects on the Indians: they got into the habit of expecting money without work; they became "lazy and dissipated" and would not take employment; and getting income without jobs "gave them a lack of confidence in their own ability to accomplish things." The depression, Collier continued, shocked Indians with the "end of the years of easy, unearned income," and now many were ready to administer their own timber programs "for the sake of wages if nothing else."[60]

Collier's approach to managing forests—like much of his Indian policy—was as much idealism as realism. He wanted Indians to have work and wages, and he believed that tribal forest industries could give all able-bodied men on timbered reservations permanent work; no extent of forestry at Flathead could accomplish that and nor did it recognize that many would not want that sort of employment. Collier began instituting Indian-conducted logging and milling operations with the aim of no longer selling the "forest wealth" as standing timber or as logs but as finished lumber, giving Indians the profit of stumpage and wages. Allotment had been a mistake and so had been dividing up the timber. Thus, Collier argued for the return of all Indian forests to community ownership. "After four centuries or more of scorn," Collier surmised, whites were coming to recognize Indian success as communal peoples and learning the limitations of applying European traditions of "higher civilization" and "private ownership" to property and natural resources.[61]

Collier believed the "community operation of Indian forests" would instill pride and valuable work skills among tribal people and he hoped it would point the way for "future development in the white civilization." This re-envisioning of forests was a vital part of Collier's overall plan for Indian natural resources. The fundamental base of that plan focused on the reacquisition of land and then systematic management of the land and resources. In the 1930s, the Indian Office began buying up property lost to non-Indian farmers, ranchers, and businessmen. BIA employees learned the mantra: the effective organization of "land, water, mankind and animal into a productive working unit must concern itself with a profound consideration of two basic economic problems, namely, (1) the conservation of natural resources, and (2) the social and industrial evolution of a people." These two goals were interrelated; the environment was of primary importance to human progress. Moreover, maintaining a "proper environment" required the principles of conservation: "the preservation of land, water, forest and forage, in a safe and entire state, the utilization of these resources for the purpose to which they were dedicated by nature, and the full enjoyment thereof, today, without destroying the promise of continued enjoyment tomorrow." Whether this "conservation" tended more to preservation or wise-use was obvious.[62]

Clearly, the BIA believed the future economic independence of Indians relied on the conservation of land and natural resources. Its language sounded like a throwback to the Progressive Era and the wise-use ideologies of those like Pinchot. For all its talk of "scientific management," "efficient administration," and "systematic programs," however, the Indian Office leaned to a more preservationist stance on natural resources. Nevertheless, tribal acquisition of abandoned, logged-over allotments, frequently located in the "very heart" of forest areas requiring consolidated management, seemed advisable. In the winter of 1934, officials began organizing "Leader Trainer Camps" on reservations for educating Indians as forest rangers, range managers, erosion experts, irrigation engineers, and general land managers. The program, under the Civilian Conservation Corps–Indian Division (CCC-ID), would educate two hundred Indians by "training on the job."[63]

In 1933-34, the Senate Committee on Indian Affairs conducted investigations into the conditions of Indians in the United States, including Indians and natural resources. The testimony indicated the conflicted aims within the Indian Office and the divergence between federal policy and the desires of Indians. Chairman of the hearings, Montana Senator Burton K. Wheeler, interrogated Flathead forest supervisor Charles Faunce on lumbering. Wheeler argued, "if you approve of the method by which [lumber companies] have cut the timber, leaving no seedlings at all… if that is according to the way the forestry department cuts timber, it is entirely different from what I understand to be the method that is generally in vogue." Wheeler's hostility was justified; reforestation and preservation of timber had not kept up with the extensive volume of cutting from 1924-1934. This revealed the lack of funding for Indian reservations, but also the BIA's inability to efficiently manage so many diverse programs on a large number of reservations.[64]

Besides the repercussions of over-harvesting, the Senate hearings raised issues of inequity in forestry employment. The Indian Office often chose whites over Indians as forest rangers, arguing that whites were educated in forestry and knew how to read and write. Senator Wheeler replied that if the BIA had gotten more Indians employed sooner, they could have trained them for the work, and thus resolved the excuse that Indians were not qualified. After all, wasn't the aim to make them able to work and support themselves? Moreover, many forestry jobs, such as scaling lumber and fire suppression, did not require a college education or even literacy. The hearings reflected the intentions of Collier, yet not only had the objectives not trickled down but field employees seemed resistant to those objectives. Senator Lynn Frazier of North Dakota chastised Faunce for failing to employ Indians at the agency sawmill. Though the depression continued to limit the amount of timber sold, it made sense for the Flathead to at least "make some money off their own timber" through wages. Frazier continued by asking if Faunce saw a problem in getting Indians to do the work. Contrary to his argument about Indians in forestry jobs, Faunce admitted that the majority were "good mechanics" and when the Indian Office used to operate the mill they utilized "Indian labor throughout." Failures in the field negated the mandates for efficiency and Indian self-support that came from above.[65]

The Senate hearings also dredged up fraudulent timber activities. From 1915-1918, the Reclamation Service had taken one half million feet of timber and seven thousand poles, fence posts, and cords of wood for constructing irrigation camps and camp use, but had never paid the Flathead tribe anything. Apparently, wise-use meant different things for federal agencies and Indians. The extensive volume of cutting had also masked non-Indian timber trespass. Albert Lemery, a tribal member, testified that, in the leaner times of the depression, people continued to slip onto allotments owned by him and his son and haul off wood. Reservation officials consistently failed to prevent this theft and never prosecuted anyone for it. The issues raised in the Senate hearings prompted more federal assistance for Flathead forestry. However, they also suggested the injustices of Indian timbering and difficulties in federal management of tribal natural resources. As Lemery concluded, "There is a lot of trouble about wood."[66]

Still, New Deal Emergency Conservation Work programs offered relief to impoverished Indians and forest protection. In 1934-35, the Indian Office allotted Flathead $325,000 for conservation projects. President Franklin D. Roosevelt authorized the expenditure of $2 million for relief and rural rehabilitation on tribal lands. That funding supported a great deal of work by the CCC-ID for the general "betterment of the Indian estate" and to alleviate the problems of overgrazing and "overcutting" of timber. The programs funded water development, fencing, range and forest improvement, construction of truck trails, and erosion control. This was Collier's vision in action; he meant to refute the idea that the "Indian problem" was "insoluble." He proclaimed, "It was insoluble so long as Indian administration, consciously or unconsciously, was bent on destroying Indian resources and Indian morale, on removing from their lives those springs of hope and energy which lead men to struggle upward."[67]

Notwithstanding the consistent difficulties of Indian administration, the New Deal proved a windfall to natural resource programs on Montana reservations. Collier was quite aware of the complications arising from the involvement of different federal agencies on tribal lands. The Soil Conservation Service, Bureau of Biological Survey, and the U.S. Forest Service of the Agriculture Department either administered or provided advice on the management of resources. And, the Indian Office had its Forest Division, Irrigation Service, and the CCC-ID doing the same.[68] Still, conservation remained crucial. In 1937, Collier instituted roadless areas on Indian lands. He contended that mechanization had spread across America, making "every nook and corner of the country a part of the machine world" and thus wiped out all "traces of the primitive." For Collier, "primitive" not only meant untarnished nature but Indian culture. He concluded, "If, on reservations where the Indians desire privacy, sizeable areas are uninvaded by roads, then it will be possible for the Indians of these tribes to maintain a retreat where they may escape from contact with white men." The order established the 125,000-acre Mission Range roadless area on the Flathead Reservation.[69]

While the Indian Office fostered its forest protection programs, it also battled for lost Flathead resources. In 1938, it sued the Polleys Lumber Company for failing to meet its contractual obligations. In 1933, the BIA let a contract to the company for the cutting of 105 million feet, but Polleys did not even cut the minimum amount the contract required. What trees it removed it did not pay for—a whopping $83,000 worth. The Indian Office sued for that amount plus $11,000 in interest. Despite the fraudulent disregard for compensation, Polleys inability to make good reflected the extent to which the depression devastated Flathead timbering.[70]

New Deal programs established a great number of natural resource management practices on Indian lands. Emergency Conservation Work Project funds created jobs for Indians to build roads, repair irrigation works, clear flammable brush and timber, plant trees, improve grazing lands, and eradicate insect pests. The Civilian Conservation Corps–Indian Division had the most profound effect on Flathead forestry. From the mid-1930s through the early 1940s, the CCC-ID funded the extensive replanting of cut-over areas and built an extensive Indian firefighting system. CCC-ID assisted the Indian Office's forestry branch in hiring and training Indians to fight fires, supplying equipment, constructing fire lookout posts, and creating fire pre-suppression policies to prevent fires from getting started in highly prone drought conditions. Flathead had one of the largest forestry staffs of any Indian reservation.[71]

The conservation of valuable forest resources demanded the support of New Deal programs, but federal funds could only go so far. The Indian Office envisioned tribal natural resources as a means to make Indians self-supporting. Over time, this goal conflicted with other BIA objectives. The steady wages of New Deal jobs at Flathead pushed Indians away from the work the Indian Office saw as most "proper," namely agriculture. The narrow focus on making Indian farmers was anachronistic. The surety of wages from non-farm work opened new avenues for subsistence, and presumably taught habits of thrift and did more to "amalgamate" Indians because agriculture, in the Jeffersonian fashion, separated them from society. While farming had been seasonal and irregular labor for many Indians, CCC-ID and the Works Progress Administration offered "careers." The BIA worried that the New

Deal would end and the battle to find employment for Indians would begin anew. CCC-ID projects and WPA relief dwindled to such an extent that Superintendent Luman W. Shotwell feared that riots for relief would break out. Still, the push to get "enrollees back to their allotments" and farming ignored that many Indians preferred other types of work.[72]

The Indian Reorganization Act of 1934 emphasized the desires of Indians, fostering new tribal natural resource policies. The Flathead constitution promoted sustained-yield management in tribal forests.[73] But, council members accused the Indian Office of stipulating forest conservation the Flathead did not want. The BIA stepped in and prevented the tribe from selling ripe timber. Tribal representative, S. C. De Mers, explained, "They have a sustained-yield program that…is a beautiful picture painted of a program, but if that program is followed much of our fine timber will be lost." At issue were limits set on cutting, and many Indians supported more extensive lumbering. Overripe, merchantable timber was subject to frost- and fire-kill. More importantly, increased timber sales meant more money for social and economic programs, the main goal of tribal natural resource programs. The sustained-yield program ignored the authority vested in the tribe by the IRA They wanted to use their resources as much as possible "without being told by the office…that we can do nothing or cannot do something."[74]

By the late 1930s, the demand for timber began to revive. Still, logging at Flathead remained at stagnant levels—with annual cutting at about ten million feet and an income of $16,000 or less—from 1932 through 1941. One Indian Office employee went so far as to assert that timber had "ceased to be an important factor in the reservation economy." Yet under its constitution, the Flathead efficiently met all tribal expenses. Moreover, the tribal council took action to capitalize on their timber resources. Daniel Lemery, the council secretary, proposed the establishment of a paper mill to furnish employment and income for the tribe. Though the commercial timber on the reservation amounted to over 900 million feet, the BIA vetoed the request. Officials argued that only a small part of the wood was suitable for making paper and the initial investment of over $1 million for machinery made the suggestion impractical. Nevertheless, the entrepreneurial spirit of the tribe prompted Commissioner Collier to comment, "Flathead definitely is clearing a way out of its particular depression."[75]

World War II production bolstered cutting to a yearly average of twenty-three million feet. However, the preservationist conservation of the Indian Office remained the keynote. In 1941, the BIA formed a cooperative agreement with the U.S. Fish and Wildlife Service. The move partnered Indian Office personnel in the forestry and grazing divisions with Fish and Wildlife scientists to investigate wildlife problems and make recommendations for conservation management measures. The plan envisioned preserving wildlife and other natural resources on Flathead that had "national importance." The agreement emphasized the maxim that wildlife—or any other resource—must "be treated as an inseparable factor in the broad unified conservation of soil, moisture, forests, and other vegetation." Wilderness and wildlife values had to be "adjusted" to gain their "proper relation" and importance next to agricultural, stockraising, lumbering, and other development ideals.[76]

These laudable efforts incited great agitation within the Flathead tribe. Although Indian Office plans focused on wildlife first, its conservation goals applied to all natural resources. On October 2, 1942, the tribal council passed game and fish regulations along the lines suggested by the BIA. However, William Zimmerman, Assistant Commissioner of Indian Affairs, charged that many Flathead did not share the "progressive attitude" towards resource conservation. The "anti-conservation sentiment" of some tribal members threatened council resolutions. The Indian Office warned that if the tribe did not pass conservation ordinances and police their own activities, the federal government would be forced to do it for them. Superintendent Shotwell charged that "radical and selfish groups" opposing the regulations were "flaunting their ability to create opposition." BIA officials missed the point. Accusing a "behind the scenes click" of obstructing "progress," they failed to realize that their influence on certain tribal council members amounted to the same thing. Regardless of the prudence of conservation measures, the Indian Office failed to credit tribal claims that they were "white men's ideas and injurious to the Indian."[77]

While the Indian Office subjected the Flathead Tribal Council and tribal members to its conservation goals, the Indians struck back. They argued that the BIA sustained-yield programs and "numerous regulations governing the sale of timber" continued to ignore tribal wishes. In 1944, the tribe passed resolutions to prevent this obstruction to what they saw as the most beneficial use of timber. Disregarding Indian Office regulations, the Flathead called for an annual maximum cut of fourteen million feet. Furthermore, the tribe alleged that if the Indian Irrigation Service could acquire and use lands—at a value of over $2,000,000—for watering crops without compensation to the tribe, then they had an equal right under the Indian Reorganization Act to flaunt BIA timbering policies.[78]

Administering Flathead natural resources—particularly water and wood—attested to the difficulty of mixing policy goals and controlling the actions of a diverse federal field force. Ideas of development and conservation revealed the entangled aims of Indian Office bureaucracy. By the mid-1940s, some officials began to concede to their dilemma in combining divergent views on natural resource management. Forests and water were not mutually exclusive. Timber had long been the basis of Flathead tribal income, but the irrigation project also played a key role in natural resource development. The Indian Office backed itself into a corner by choosing one over the other; it liquidated timber assets to fund irrigation when Indians wanted the income for other purposes. Lacking agreement upon a common goal, the Indian Office simply did not have a coherent policy to develop tribal resources. After the war, the BIA began letting lumber contracts to the highest bidder. The Flathead argued that one large white operator might "freeze out" smaller Indian operators, and rejected Office policy for a bidding process on tribal timber. While the Indian Office was torn between profit and preservation, the Flathead wrestled with maximum profit versus Indian control.[79]

When the Flathead took the federal government to court in the 1950s in the Indian Claims Commission, timber was a key concern. At issue was not only wood sold from existing tribal lands but the production lost from lands ceded in the nineteenth century. In short, when the Flathead accepted the cession of lands they also gave up a vast amount of timber at a fraction of its value. Because the government had accepted excessive timbering and trespass in the nineteenth century on public lands—including lands ceded by the Flathead—they had proven themselves negligent in managing natural resources in a manner that reflected the true value of forests. E. O. Fuller, a consultant to tribal attorneys in the Flathead case, made an astounding argument. Timber on the reservation plus that ceded in nineteenth-century treaties exceeded forty billion feet. Deducting the tribal land that remained in Indian ownership after treaty cessions left fourteen million acres. In the cases of timber trespass on public domain that the federal government actually tried in court, it assessed that land at a value of $1.25 an acre—an astronomical figure of $21 million. Despite that sum, the value of timber lost amounted to over $100 million. The federal government, no matter its role in guiding American progress, certainly failed to account for the vast natural resources that it gave away without regard to the public—or Indian—good.[80]

Assessing the successes and failures of Flathead forestry and timbering requires a careful consideration of the dynamics of both culture and economics. From the early 1880s through 1945, loggers cut over 880 million board feet of timber and available records show the Flathead received $3.5 million in timber income from 1910 to 1945. As John Collier indicated, the "Indian forest problem" was a consequence "of the whole Indian land problem." Undoubtedly, the Dawes Allotment Act of 1887 and succeeding federal policies for making Indians into yeoman farmers accelerated the sale of timber when making way for farming; the government also neglected the benefits of timber when it did not fit with agricultural goals. As Collier surmised, "The results have proved again how dangerous it is to try to solve problems by theories not soundly based on the facts of life and nature." In one sense, per capita payments from timbering represented a "false economy." But the termination of lumbering, tribal income from timber, and the "collapse of employment" during the Great Depression could hardly have been predicted. Still, J. P. Kinney argued, it seemed an utter failure that federal officials, white contractors, and tribes "couldn't see far enough ahead to realize it would be better for the Indians to hold those lands as forest lands, rather than to have them cut." Kinney concluded, "I've always said that the main fault of the Indians is that they're just more human than white folks. They didn't want their money invested in future forestry when they could get it for use now." Kinney's analysis did not tell the whole story.[81]

It is widely believed that Indians were, and are, strict environmentalists, conservationists, even preservationists, but in many cases this perception is false or misleading. Conservation meant different things to Indians and non-Indians. Many federal policymakers saw Indian reservations as the last refuges for the conservation of wildlife, forests, and watersheds in a West with rapidly diminishing natural resources. On tribal lands, they often equated conservation with "preservation," rather than wise-use. Many Indians, on the other hand, stuck to the wise-use ideology, and many times went beyond the idea of balancing economic gain with preservation. Most Indians had experienced little but poverty and despair since the Dawes Act. The history of Flathead timbering challenges the concept of the "ecological Indian." When forced to decide between saving a few trees and reaping a profit for their tribe that promised security, there was no choice at all. Indians often chose utilization over preservation. Managing Flathead forests involved more than economic and cultural values. The actions of the Flathead after the Indian Reorganization Act and the formation of their tribal government revealed it was also about control, deciding who had the authority to set the value of wood. Increasing economic and political independence in the mid-twentieth century enabled the Flathead to begin unseating the federal government from its reign over tribal forests.

# Chapter 3

# The "Indian Muscle Shoals"

# Power Development
# on the Flathead Reservation

Like irrigation and timbering, hydroelectric power development on the Flathead Reservation provoked great disputes. Power not only represented electricity for powering homes, agency buildings, and off-reservation enterprises, but it became a symbol of the battle to control tribal natural resources. Spanning a period of almost eighty years, the contest over power, and who would receive the electric and economic benefits of that power, exemplified Flathead challenges to federal natural resource policy on tribal lands. The Flathead power project—the "Indian Muscle Shoals"—was the largest hydroelectric project on any Indian reservation. Investors, engineers, and power companies across the nation competed for the spoils. Disregarding Flathead rights and desires, many non-Indians believed they could make "better use" of that power. Of all the environmental assets at Flathead, hydroelectric power epitomized the lengths the federal government and non-Indians would go to in order to exploit Indian resources.

With its abundant rivers and the elevation gradient those streams followed, the Flathead Reservation offered great opportunities for hydropower development. From the beginning, the Reclamation and Indian Bureaus recognized this potential. In the midst of planning the Flathead Irrigation Project, the two agencies lobbied congress for aid. In 1904 and 1906, it passed legislation setting aside power sites on the reservation "in the interest of the Flathead tribe." Meanwhile, Indian Office forestry employees and other conservationists linked hydroelectricity to the wider milieu of natural resources. Preserving forests meant protecting waterpower. They connected forests to the "water supply in all its phases": irrigation, inland navigation, floods, drainage, soil conservation, public health, domestic consumption, and power.[1]

Nevertheless, great debate existed between preservation, conservation for the benefit of the Flathead, or putting natural resources to more extensive use for the benefit of all Americans. During the last few years of the Theodore Roosevelt presidency, Interior Secretary James Garfield withdrew lands "for the purpose of checking the acquisition of valuable power sites in the mountain regions of the West by syndicates, which were believed to be attempting to monopolize all the available power possibilities in certain regions." The threat of hydroelectric "power monopoly" required closer attention to conservation and the public good. Though the original plans for the power project at Flathead only contemplated a small development to augment pumping for irrigation, the massive potential for electricity loomed large in the minds of many Americans. A number of western senators argued that Roosevelt's conservation policies hampered economic development. Many westerners wanted "an influx of capital," not preservation of resources. Despite the grumbling, the *New York Post* surmised, "the nation is coming to see that it cannot eat the cake and have it too." However, by 1909, with Richard A. Ballinger as Interior Secretary, the prospect of conserving power sites on western streams became a considerably more disputed subject.[2]

Because it was intimately tied to forest issues, waterpower became a part of the conflict between Chief U.S. Forester Gifford Pinchot and Secretary Ballinger. Pinchot argued for the reservation of forests, and the "highly important water powers" within them, for "public benefit and use." At issue was the protection of forests and waterpower "against corporate absorption." Ballinger opened lands to settlement that Secretary Garfield had withdrawn for conservation purposes. The lands contained power sites, and Ballinger's action added to the potential of them being "gobbled up" by trusts that had already acquired a good portion of the water available for power in the West.[3] The Ballinger-Pinchot dispute highlighted the increasing role of "federal bureaucracy" in natural resource management. However, the quarrel suggested deeper repercussions. Generally, Pinchot argued for a greater federal role, while Ballinger emphasized the importance of private enterprise. This contributed to a schizophrenic power policy; the Flathead Reservation was a showcase for the split-personality of natural resource administration. Without a definitive plan, hydroelectric power at Flathead became a political football bouncing between federal control, corporate interests, and Indian rights.[4]

In the meantime, the Indian and Reclamation Bureaus focused on putting power to use. From May of 1909 to December of 1911, the Reclamation Service dug the Newell Tunnel on the south side of Flathead

Lake. Crews drilled the 1,800-foot tunnel through hard limestone. The work moved slow—a mere two feet a day—and required 262,325 drills, or 8 drills per foot of advance. Water flowing through the tunnel would power pumps to irrigate farms. To ensure Indian rights, a congressional act of June 25, 1910, safeguarded the "water interests" on tribal lands opened to white settlers prior to completion of the irrigation project. More important, the act reserved power sites from settlement to secure future development of power for other uses besides watering crops.[5]

White settlement at Flathead conflicted with power development. Two major problems arose. Prior to the appraisal and classification of the reservation, the Indian Office made allotments to tribal members. Later, the BIA discovered that some tracts fell within power sites needed by the Reclamation Service, requiring the exchange of those lands for lieu allotments elsewhere on the reservation. In turn, after the opening of the reservation in 1910, whites settled lands that had not been classified. This resulted in two conflicts. Some of those lands would be designated as power reserves, necessitating the removal of whites to other tracts. In addition, because certain Flathead Indians required new allotments, the Indian Office felt the protection of the interests of the Indians demanded that they receive

Workers on the Flathead Lake dam. L to R: Louie Ninepipe, Eneas Inmee.

lands already settled—and sometimes improved—by whites. This was no small problem. The land "conflicts" involved close to thirty thousand acres and invited frequent cases of trespass. Many non-Indians, like Dave E. Parry, squatted on tracts needed for Indians in lieu of allotments on reservoir sites. Parry, in a hasty attempt to secure title, tilled and made improvements in the hope that the BIA would not favor the Indians. Parry's actions prevented Flathead Clara Morais from taking possession of her property. In all such cases, the Indian Office requested the assistance of the U.S. Attorney for the "speedy removal" of trespassers.[6]

The conflict over the opening and settlement of the reservation became a key obstacle to the development of natural resources and the protection of Indian rights. When the Indian Office sent William Ketcham to investigate, he concluded, "The confusion and complications could hardly be more and greater than they have been." The "lack of isolation" from the affairs of white settlers threatened systematic management of Indians and resources at Flathead. In 1912, the Interior Secretary surmised, "It exposes the Indian and the Indians' property to the cupidity of white men, which interferes on every hand and at every turn with the successful and efficient administration of Indian affairs." The "great and perplexing problems of public policy," including "water-power sites of great potential value," demanded prompt action by the Indian Office to ensure proper disposition and development. Between 1909 and 1914, the Interior Secretary withdrew 50,000 acres within the reservation from settlement for proposed waterpower and reservoir sites. Though the secretary later released many of these lands, the BIA's inability to prevent trespass and properly administer allotment wreaked havoc. Sorting out lands designated for power sites, Indian allotments, and "surplus" sections for settlement created deep rifts between the Flathead and whites and between resource development and protection.[7]

The waterpower issue required the Indian Office to negotiate between the demands of whites and the rights of Indians. Debate emerged over the proper use or value of land within power sites. Frank Bailey, a white resident of the reservation, criticized BIA management of power reserves on the south side of Flathead Lake. The Reclamation Service fenced up the reserve with barbed wire, preventing stock owned by both Indians and whites from watering at the river, and "thus working a great injustice and hardship on the whole community." Bailey argued, "I am one of those who differ with our Conservation friends, and I earnestly advocate permitting the People [to] use our natural resources...and permitting no one person, corporation, or concern whatever to...deprive all the people from deriving any benefit from them whatever." Conversely, the BIA received over fifty letters from whites in late-1913 demanding that it secure appropriations for

Plasí Cocowee

power development to bolster "irrigation so greatly needed" by settlers. Reclamation Director Frederick Newell found the demands disconcerting. The Reclamation Service had developed the Newell Tunnel to supplement irrigation as well as "hold for the benefit of the Indians or of the public" the "valuable water power." In effect, the letters were "insistent claims" emphasizing the value of irrigated farming over other important benefits to be derived from power development.[8]

The Indian Office faced difficult choices on Flathead natural resource management. It needed to balance the demands of irrigation, farming, power development, and natural resource protection. In turn, it had to juggle the interests of whites with the rights of Indians. Irrigation and waterpower were intimately connected but also served different aims. The power plans for the Flathead Irrigation Project initially included "nothing more than a modest irrigation plant" funded by the sale of surplus tribal lands and timber. The Reclamation and Indian Bureaus wanted to supply irrigation as well as generate income from tribal power resources. By 1914, the "scheme of irrigating and producing power" had grown to "gigantic dimensions," requiring millions of dollars for completion. The massive funds and great length of time required to build the irrigation and power works posed serious concerns. Though Indian land and timber financed the projects, the Chief Engineer of the Indian Irrigation Service admitted that a middle-aged Indian residing on the reservation at the time would probably not live to see any income generated from tribal power resources. In fact, the magnitude of the scheme had "gone so far beyond what any one would expect the Indian to do or anyone would expect to do for the Indian," that it only seemed fair to have the government finance it rather than the Flathead. This was quite a noble proposition; yet managing natural resources did not always live up to that sort of equity.[9]

The economic, philosophical, and cultural complications of water-power development delayed progress throughout the first two decades of the twentieth century. Besides the construction of the Newell Tunnel and pumps to augment irrigation, the Indian Office took little action. In 1918, Flathead Superintendent Theodore Sharp continued to protest against BIA failures to compensate the tribe for irrigation and waterpower. The Flathead had "good reason to complain" about the appropriation of a large acreage of tribal land for reservoir, camp, and power sites and other reserves for the reclamation project without any reimbursement to the tribe. Nevertheless, officials intended to generate some profit for the tribe from power sites. The income did not come from electricity but from leasing the property for grazing. The failure of congress to pass a national "water-power bill" also militated against hydroelectric development at Flathead. Most private companies did not want to take the risk before the federal government established legislation regulating hydropower. In 1920, congress passed the Federal Power Act establishing the Federal Power Commission and setting the guidelines for power development. The Montana Power Company had already leased some "Interior Department lands" in the state, but with the passage of the act it immediately made application for development on the Flathead Reservation. Though unrecognized at the time, this move inaugurated what would become a massive controversy spanning sixty-five years.[10]

In the 1920s, a hydropower craze swept across the country. Power resources not only offered immense revenue but would confer great authority upon those who controlled them. Western power development divided the nation, the federal bureaucracy, and local communities. States, corporations, and individuals battled for the spoils that promised to stream from waterpower. The Reclamation Service suffered the brunt of these contests. In 1923, Interior Secretary Hubert Work played his hand at influencing the situation. Rumors swelled across the West that Work, realizing the great profit and potential of waterpower, wanted to rid the Reclamation Service of "expert technical men" and replace them with "business men." This was more than a federal power struggle, or a "political pork barrel," but a brawl between private enterprise and government control. The bureaucratic manifestation of this fight began with division between Reclamation Director Arthur Powell Davis and Secretary Work.[11]

Harnessing hydroelectricity meant a power play in the Interior Department. Apparently, Davis sacrificed himself at the altar of the public good. From the early 1920s on, Davis began intimating a corporate conspiracy to wrest control of federal power sites from the Interior Department and Reclamation Service. Davis partly interpreted this as an assault against the competency of the Reclamation Service, which he claimed had "become so efficient that it is a thorn in the flesh of some of the large corporations that don't want any proof that the Government can handle affairs efficiently and economically." He alleged that private companies claimed that no government organization could be "economical and efficient," and the success of the Reclamation Service was a "fly in their ointment." However, much greater motives lay behind the assault on Davis. Western interests, particularly electric companies, wanted the income from waterpower. These desires were most apparent in relation to the proposed Boulder Dam in Nevada and the prospects of damming the Columbia River in Washington state. Davis supported "public ownership and operation of public utilities" so that Americans, via the government, could profit from the resources. In 1923, Work forced the resignation of Davis.[12] It appeared that the loss of this "brave" engineer meant the "great natural resources of the West [were] to go for a song." It seemed like the Ballinger-Pinchot controversy all over again.[13]

The national outrage had local repercussions. Work replaced the "conservation expert of the government" with former Idaho Governor and banker, D. W. Davis, a "practical politician" and businessman, "whose business [was] frequently politics." No doubt, Secretary Work "was a good deal of a 'grouch' and a difficult man to get along with," but western politicians, such as Senator Lawrence C. Phipps of Colorado, wanted the removal of Davis. Phipps, a shareholder in the Southern Sierra Power Company, had his hands in both politics and profit from hydroelectric power. Work traveled to Montana in 1923 to inspect irrigation projects and potential power sites. While there, he heard complaints against Davis and the Reclamation Service. The "hammering the Secretary got from the press," public, and engineering societies added to the results of a "Fact Finding Commission" appointed by Work that "failed to substantiate his malicious charges." The commission forced Work to replace D. W. Davis with engineer Elwood Mead. For all of A. P. Davis' efforts to ensure public benefit from western power resources, the conflict in the Interior Department—as well as its relations with private companies—did not foreshadow efficient and smooth progress at Flathead.[14]

The waterpower play at Flathead began to simmer in 1925. As the uses and benefits of energy began to unfold, the currents of conflict among reservation residents increased. While it seemed that white settlers, Indians, and businessmen had equal interests in power development, as the *Ronan Pioneer* admitted, they did "not always agree." The "chief bones of contention" focused on the "disposal of the Newell Tunnel" and the various power sites. The *Pioneer* summarized the "divided opinion": "The Indians claim that this power belongs to them. The Water Users' Association claims that the Reclamation Service filed on this power for the Flathead Project, and spent more than $100,000 developing it, and that it belongs to the water users, Indian and white alike." After all, the project was what made development and success possible at Flathead. Thus, if the power belonged to the project, the Indians should merely "share in the benefits along with the white settlers." The editors of the *Pioneer* neglected two important points. First, whites benefited more from the irrigation project than the Flathead; assigning the power to project ownership rather than to the Indians portended further inequity. More to the point, most white farmers had not or could not pay their construction charges and yet they still wanted the value of power sites. Settlers felt they should not relinquish their "rights to this power, merely being reimbursed" for the money spent by

Flathead Lake dam worker.

the Reclamation Service on the tunnel. Thus, they wanted the government to build the project and not a private corporation that might deliver more benefits to Indians that white irrigation interests.[15]

Hydroelectric development at Flathead rested on conflicts about what constituted the "public" interest. Was power or irrigation more important? Should Indians or whites benefit more, or should there be a balance between the two? In 1926, congress appropriated $575,000 for the Flathead Irrigation Project, including $395,000 for power development. The Indian Office reported that pumping water for irrigation would not be "economically sound under normal conditions," but the Flathead case raised two issues that made the proposition feasible. First, the Reclamation and Indian Bureaus had built a massive irrigation project involving an expenditure of millions of dollars, yet the system produced too little water to meet the demands of farmers. Next, there existed "a large and unused water power" to provide needed electrical energy. The reasoning seemed to be that untapped resources lay dormant, so why not exploit them? The BIA proposed a small power plant sufficient to produce 6,000 horsepower for pumping. The Federal Power Commission vetoed the suggestion, arguing that it would impede full development. In lieu of that plan, the Rocky Mountain Power Company, a subsidiary of the Montana Power Company, proposed the construction of Kerr Dam at the south end of Flathead Lake for providing 120,000 horsepower.[16]

The strategy provoked disagreement and disgruntlement. Indian Commissioner Charles H. Burke contested the commission's decision. He argued that, in 1909, the Indian Office initiated power utilization, via the Newell Tunnel, and it never abandoned the proposition. Thus, the Flathead Indians had never relinquished any rights in and to the development, negating the jurisdiction of the commission over the project. The Flathead Tribal Council seconded the contention that the property belonged to the Indians, opposed the contract of the Montana Power Company, and argued that Burke could only act in behalf of tribal wishes. Moreover, conflict arose over the duty of the power. Many settlers and government officials argued that thorough and successful irrigation remained the objective. Irrigating some lands would cost close to $100 an acre—four times what was feasible—paying the excess expenses of irrigation with revenues from the power plant. As one engineer concluded, "The proposed repayment basis is an exceedingly liberal one and it is unfortunate that it is incorporated in the same plan as the proposed power scheme." Most Flathead agreed.[17]

Despite these objections, congress and the Federal Power Commission moved forward on the contract with Montana Power. In February 1927, the parties agreed to build the power plant and dam. It required company reimbursement to the federal government for the cost of constructing the

Newell Tunnel, and granted to the government, as trustee for the Flathead, a permit for fifty years of operation with payment of one dollar per annual average horsepower.[18] Many Flathead residents, particularly white settlers, welcomed the plans. Government development of a smaller capacity plant stood in the way of utilizing the full power potential. Between the completion of the Newell Tunnel in 1911 and the bigger plans consummated in 1927, white residents acquiesced to the smaller enterprise out of "despair" that nothing would be done at all. In an address at the town of Ronan, on the reservation, Montana Senator Thomas J. Walsh declared that maximum development would move forward. Serious controversy continued about whether corporations or the government should develop the power. The plans had a price tag of $8 million, and, to many congressmen, that was an unacceptable federal expenditure. The project shockingly surpassed any other natural resource gratuity the federal government had ever offered to private interests in the history of the West.[19]

Funding aside, what the residents of the reservation really worried about was the distribution of economic benefits. In 1909 and 1920, legislation promised that the power sites and all royalties belonged to the Flathead tribe. Walsh admitted that this was very "disappointing" to whites, but "general opinion" prevailed that the government "robbed the Indians in the past and that they were mistreated." Many federal officials saw profits from power as the means to reconcile the long tradition of non-Indian exploitation of other tribal natural resources. Nevertheless, the government would not cheat whites out of their just reward. Hydroelectric development meant that close to $8 million would flow into the community, partly in the form of jobs. The project would also produce additional markets for farm goods, spur the development of new manufacturing enterprises, and bring in more settlers who would demand services. Quoting poet John J. Ingalls, Walsh concluded, "opportunity knocks once and never comes again. I feel that opportunity is before you now."[20]

The power rights belonged to the Flathead, but the "Indian Muscle Shoals" involved "trickery" that surpassed any scheme ever undertaken for federal natural resource development on tribal lands. Montana Senator Burton K. Wheeler and A. A. Grorud, attorney for the Flathead tribal council, discovered collusion between Indian Commissioner Charles Burke and the Montana Power Company. Apparently, the Company, abetted by Burke, setup a "pow wow" with four "old chiefs" at Hamilton, Montana, over one hundred miles from the reservation. The Indians "were furnished with ample eats and drinks, including intoxicating liquors, and…they were kept well supplied with liquor." Under this influence, company officials induced the Indians to sign a petition addressed to Burke requesting that the

Montana Power Company be allowed to develop Flathead power. The tribal council knew nothing of this "irregular action" by the four Indians, nor did the rest of the tribe. Burke's "hasty action" and its secrecy indicated that the Flathead would never have consented to the scheme.[21]

For all the frankness and sentimentality of his address at Ronan, Walsh did not have the full story. He declared that he had nothing against the Montana Power Company except that it monopolized natural resource development in Montana. Walsh hoped some other company would come into the state and "divide up the business with it," but apparently no other company asked for a permit. However, in the fall of 1927, Walter H. Wheeler, a Minnesota businessman and engineer, made a proposal to construct the power project. The Flathead tribal council charged that Montana Power had "refused to deal with the Indians openly and in a businesslike manner," resorting to "trickery, secretive and underhanded methods, and ha[d] aided and conspired with the Indian Bureau" to deprive them of the proceeds from power. They protested the confiscation of their "property and rights which legally, morally, and of right" belonged to them. In November, the Flathead tribal council, guided by the votes of the tribe, rejected the proposal of Montana Power and accepted the contract with Wheeler.[22]

The actions of Burke and the Flathead tribal council produced great upheaval. Though the power and its benefits theoretically belonged to the tribe, the Interior Secretary had the ultimate authority to decide who developed it. Despite Flathead support for Walter Wheeler, federal officials were uncertain how to handle the situation. The Montana Power Company maintained that Wheeler's "propaganda" had little bearing because the Federal Power Commission had already granted it the contract. Nevertheless, with two competitors in the picture and to ensure proper development, the Interior Department requested that Montana Power supply complete surveys and economic data on their plans. The request tied up the project and would delay construction for several years. The holdup would cost Montana Power profits, but it also bought time for the government to deliberate on the problems hindering the project. The Burke debacle enraged senators and congressmen. In Senate hearings, Burton K. Wheeler informed Assistant Commissioner E. B. Meritt that he and other senators had to fight "to see that the Indians get what is justly coming to them, when you have a department that is supposed to act as the guardian of the Indians but instead…have stood silently by and seen the resources of the Indian demolished." Senator Wheeler accused the BIA of idly allowing the Flathead to be dispossessed of vast natural resources even though the treaty of 1855 guaranteed tribal rights. Now, the Indian Office "promoted the misappropriation of the Flathead water power." The past contained lessons that BIA administrators refused to learn.[23]

While the power dispute primarily involved local interests at the Flathead Reservation, the implications of the contest extended throughout the West. As early as 1923, Reclamation Director A. P. Davis had realized that western businessmen sought to wrest control of power development from the federal government. Serious conflict existed between Flathead and Columbia River basin interests. Though one Montana Power Company official referred to it as a "tempest in the teapot," the battle for waterpower was no trivial matter. The water that the Kerr Dam would hold back at Flathead Lake flowed into the Flathead River, then emptied into the Clark Fork, and ultimately ended up in the Columbia River watershed. Conceivably, developing power at Flathead Lake might render the available storage capacity of Lake Pend'Oreille insufficient for the Columbia Basin project. Davis believed that Interior Secretary Hubert Work had forced his resignation partly to meet the demands of Columbia Basin interests. Controlling waterpower in the West was a titanic opportunity, and a tempest that shattered the confines of a mere "teapot."[24]

The power issue also created significant rifts among the Flathead Indians. By 1929, the subject had divided the tribe into two groups. One, headed by the tribal council, favored Walter Wheeler. The other group sided with the application of the Rocky Mountain Power Company. While the tribal council had more organization, made "considerable more noise," and wrote more letters on the matter, a larger majority seemed to support the Montana Power proposition. During the winter some Indians circulated a petition for that plan, which advised, "We are told that in two or three years, at the latest, our timber will all be gone, and then we will have no source of revenue unless we lease the power site.... If we are to get this site leased...we must act at once." Three-quarters of the Indians signed it. However, Superintendent Charles Coe reported all this information, and many questioned his honesty in the matter. The divided opinion had as much to do with outside as internal influences.[25]

Debate over Flathead raised serious questions about federal control of power development. Officials within the Federal Power Commission abetted the fraudulent activities of the Montana Power Company. The accounting division, "heart of the commission's structure," controlled the expenditures made by contractors. The chief accountant approved payments used for "urging opinion" to the company's "side of the issue." Though the accountant deemed the expenditures improper, pressure from the executive secretary, who gave the "tentative award" of the Flathead development to Montana Power, forced the disbursement. In a 1929 investigation of the charges, the Interstate Commerce Commission (I.C.C.) made inquiries into why higher officials overruled recommendations made by the accountant. The I.C.C. reported that Rocky Mountain Power spent considerable sums on propaganda, "made donations to churches, clubs, athletic associations, and various organizations; spent sums of money to entertain certain conventions, and even defrayed the funeral expenses of a certain man," and "used other improper means of influencing" the Flathead. Despite the company's efforts to sway Indian opinion, the chief engineer for Montana Power stated at Federal Power Commission hearings that "the Indians should not be given any payments for the Flathead site, since the water belongs to the people of Montana." In its scams to exploit Flathead power, the company exploited the Indians.[26]

The stock market crash of 1929 and the ensuing Great Depression prompted further investigations into hydroelectric development at Flathead. Many hoped to put the project on a more organized and equitable basis. The house and senate committees on Indian affairs initiated legislation authorizing the Interior Secretary "to develop power and to lease for power purposes structures on Indian irrigation projects." The profit derived from the leasing of surplus power not needed for irrigation pumping would go to the credit of the project. Congressmen envisioned this arrangement as providing "considerable advantage from a financial angle." Many did

"Mucking" or clearing blast debris during dam construction.

not want any power development that might "impair the efficiency of the irrigation project." On the other hand, some politicians, like Montana Senators Burton K. Wheeler and Thomas J. Walsh, demanded that congress and the Federal Power Commission think of the Indians before watering crops; they insisted that Montana Power pay the Flathead a royalty. This unprecedented demand extended the controversy to new limits.[27]

Conspiracy and deception in Flathead power development ran rampant through the Indian Office. Senate hearings held in March of 1930 exposed the extremity of the problem. Assistant Commissioner J. Henry Scattergood claimed the "interest of the Indian Bureau in this matter has been to represent the Indians" and that "the proceeds from a power site on a reservation should go to the Indians." However, since at least 1925 the BIA proposed to divert the proceeds from power generated at the Newell Tunnel to the federal government to cover the costs of irrigation construction. The congressional appropriation bill of 1927 on Flathead power revealed the "incapacity and recklessness" of the Indian Office, it definitely having "withheld from the records the facts which would have proved that the pumping project was not only impractical but was fictitious." The BIA "misstated the acreage which could be served by gravity water," misrepresented the time when the pumping would be needed, and lied about the market for power. Its "whole presentation to Congress was not only incompetent but was misleading and false."[28]

The allegations fingered Flathead Superintendent Charles Coe, irrigation project engineer C. J. Moody, employees of Montana Power, and a coterie of Indians. Moody "spent his entire time for months" engineering the "fantastic Newell Tunnel scheme" to confiscate profits from power to pay irrigation costs rather than the Indians. Resolutions of the tribal council charged that Montana Power had for three years been a "corrupting, blackmailing and unscrupulous influence...paying money to irresponsible Indians and dishonest whites, circulating fake petitions...and stopping at nothing short of murder in its determination to get possession of the Flathead power sites on terms disadvantageous to the Flathead Tribe." In his annual report, Coe reported that the Indian Office should be "congratulated on the extremely favorable terms that were obtained for the Indians." However, in his agency office, Coe organized a fake organization called the "Flathead Indian Association" to deliver tribal power sites "by hook or crook" to Montana Power. The association, "officered by hireling Indians" of the company, issued statements to congress about tribal wishes on power that were "diametrically opposed to and misrepresenting the real action of the Tribe." The company bribed five Indians to do their bidding, two of which received indictments and were currently serving time in penitentiaries. Though Interior Secretary Ray Lyman Wilbur, Indian Commissioner Charles J. Rhoads, and Assistant Commissioner Scattergood knew about this activity, they defended Coe's reputation and actions as superintendent, and denounced the authority of the tribal council to oppose the "power monopoly." Thus, as John Collier surmised, "the destruction of the Tribe's collective life has gone forward apace."[29]

The dilemma largely stemmed from the decision to award the hydroelectric contract to the Montana Power Company. It did not take much to realize that a "power-monopoly" controlled Montana. Instead of acting in the interest of the Flathead Indians or public consumers of electricity, some federal officials favored an "interlocking chemical-fertilizer-metallurgical monopoly." Montana Power used its "dummy" company, Rocky Mountain Power, to evade government regulation. John D. Ryan headed both Montana Power and the Anaconda Copper Company. The American Power and Light Company, one of four huge holding companies in the United States, owned Ryan's businesses. In turn, a vaster organization, the Electric Bond and Share Company, controlled, but did not own, American Power. In a series of articles on the debacle, John Collier claimed, "The [federal] officials are danced as puppets by these mighty showmen."[30]

The full facts of the case came out in Senate hearings. The power project included five different sites along the Flathead River that could generate an estimated 214,000 horsepower. Rocky Mountain Power and Walter H. Wheeler proposed separate plans for developing the sites. Wheeler's plan had a higher cost per horsepower developed and was close to $1.25 million more than Rocky Mountain Power's proposition. However, Wheeler intended to fund his scheme with outside investments from companies that would attract industries to the region. This would bring the Flathead new opportunities for "remunerative employment" and create improved markets for farm and other Indian products. Those new industries would compete with Anaconda Copper and deflate the monopolization of natural resources in Montana. As aforementioned, the Flathead tribe and Wheeler agreed to a contract in 1927, but federal officials overruled that decision in favor of Montana Power. The final option had been government development, but the eight-million-dollar price tag portended a federal fiasco.[31]

Walter H. Wheeler took the stand at the senate hearings in late March of 1930. He wanted to show that the Indian Office and Federal Power Commission favored the Montana corporation even though his development would provide more revenue to the tribe. He claimed the Interior Secretary applied a "set-up of proposed rental charges" to his plans that handicapped his ability as a competitive bidder and had "the effect of granting the sites to the Montana Power Co. at a minimum rental to the Flathead tribe." Moreover,

L to R: Plasí Cocowee, Baptiste Pierre (killed during construction of the dam),
Eneas Inmee, Louie Ninepipe.

he argued that granting the license to Rocky Mountain Power would furnish 200,000 horsepower to the company when it already monopolized a similar amount at other undeveloped sites in the state. This would give the Montana syndicate the ability to dominate power development for the next fifty years and would effectively shut out all independent power interests from the state. The Flathead power sites were located at "the heart of one of the richest and most varied mineral areas in the United States." Within 125 miles, three hundred million tons of phosphate existed and only awaited the power to mine it. Wheeler argued that this made Flathead power marketable so long as the capitalization of the power was not inflated. However, over fifty-two percent of Montana Power's capitalization was "water." Wheeler contended that the company's inflated capital structure would prevent it from selling power cheap enough to attract new chemical and metallurgical industries.[32]

Interior and Indian Office officials asserted that they had no intention of awarding contracts to Flathead power without a proposition that would "wear well." Their estimates of value revealed underbidding by both competitors. A War Department report to the Federal Power Commission advised that the developer should be charged based on the amount of energy produced. This seemingly wise choice was inequitable. Because Montana Power intended to generate less power, Wheeler's proposition would automatically seem inflated. Though the BIA did not like the undervalued returns proposed by the competitors, it sided with Montana Power assuming that the BIA could establish a more economically beneficial rate structure. Moreover, it was tired of the hassle. In a conversation with Wheeler in late December of 1929, Assistant Commissioner Scattergood urged Wheeler to eliminate himself from competition and make a deal with Montana Power to become a minority stockholder in the company. Scattergood warned Wheeler, "Don't burn all your bridges behind you." Combining would end the competition. However, Scattergood later claimed that it was an "offhand joke," contending, "I didn't recommend anything from a public standpoint.... There is no public interest going to suffer here, because we hold the whip hand." He declared that he wanted Wheeler to come out a winner and also "fully protect the interests of the Indians." Despite those claims, it certainly seemed that a "public interest"—the Flathead—might suffer.[33]

The debate over awarding the contract to Rocky Mountain Power camouflaged other serious issues. Though not a disinterested party, the testimony of John Collier of the American Indian Defense Association provided thorough evidence of deception. The War Department report that established the rate structures used "fake data and fake computations," indicating a seventy-five percent decrease in the rentals to be received by the Flathead tribe. In Federal Power Commission hearings, Montana Power estimated its gross revenue was nearly forty percent less than the proper figure. However, the War Department report disregarded that in favor of the low figure reported by the company. The department claimed it intended to look after the Indian's "equitable rights," yet its recommendations would cut their income nearly in half.[34] Thus, Collier argued that the War Department fashioned a scandalous set-up that proved "either an extreme incompetence or a willful and strangely rash juggling of arithmetic, misstatement of facts of record and of acreage, and arbitrary and false construction of law." Moreover, all of this "jugglery" favored Montana Power over the Flathead Indians.[35]

Like some horrendous virus, the avaricious fight for control of power at Flathead infected almost everyone involved. The problems transcended "local politics." As Collier charged, the BIA had reached an "extreme of active tolerance of, if not collusion in, the Montana Power Co.'s use of Indians corrupted by Montana Power Co. money, to influence the Federal Power Commission, the Secretary of the Interior, and Congress." Superintendent Coe and other agency officials conspired with "bought

Indians." In exasperation, Senator Burton K. Wheeler wondered why BIA
policy did not "encourage the decent and respectable Indians" rather than
promote the interests of "crooked Indians." Senator Wheeler, and many
others, recognized that the object of hydroelectric development should be
new industries, new development, and new markets. That would not only
benefit the Flathead but whites as well. The fact was that Montana Power
was great strides ahead of Walter Wheeler in planning and financing. As
Senator Thomas Walsh concluded, it seemed to make the most business
sense—for the Indians, the public, and the irrigation project—to have the
company develop power. The Indian Office had the "double responsibility"
of protecting tribal rights via power rentals and ensuring the success of
the irrigation project for non-Indians. In 1930, the Interior Department
finalized the contract for the development and sale of Flathead power to the
company.[36]

The agreement with Rocky Mountain and Montana Power seemed
to ensure success and economic security for the Flathead. The company
would construct the power sites and received a fifty-year lease to market the
electricity. In return, the tribe would receive $60,000 per year to $175,000 at
the end of a twenty-year sliding scale period, generating close to $3 million
for the rental of the sites. Quite possibly, this was the first time in U.S.
history that Indians were compensated with royalties. This initial contract
only covered the first power site, with another four awaiting a demonstration
of efficiency by Montana Power.[37]

With the deepening of the depression the flush prospects withered.
Rocky Mountain Power paid the Flathead tribe $1,000 monthly rental
for occupancy and use and storage of power. Once the plant reached
commercial operation that fee would jump to the $60,000 figure. The tribe
staked their economic security on employment from building Kerr Dam.
In April 1931, a few months after starting construction, the company
discontinued all work, announcing that the stoppage would last at least a
year or even longer. The suspension was a severe blow to employment and
rental income prospects. The Indian Office appreciated the impediment
of the depression, but needed to guarantee the interests of the Flathead.
The initial three-year contract required completion by 1934, but the BIA
extended the due date until 1935. Assistant Commissioner Scattergood
asserted that the BIA's "broader responsibilities," particularly safeguarding
Indian interests and revenue, required new contractual terms. The conditions
for extension required the company to make payments to the tribe as if the
project had been completed. The irrigation project would not be responsible
for the increased cost of pumping because the power development was not
finished, and the company was required to supply electricity at the same

rates as if the project was finished. However, in a sudden reversal in 1932, the BIA granted the company a reduction from $60,000 per year to $1,000 per month in rental rates if Montana Power would repay the debt at the time of completion. In February of 1933, the Indian Office extended the "moratorium" an additional year.[38]

The delays produced serious protest on the reservation. The irrigation districts within the Flathead Project demanded underground water, which required electrical pumps for delivery. Since the power company could not provide that service, farmers requested that the work be completed by federal agencies as with other federal natural resource projects under New Deal agencies. John Collier, now the Commissioner of Indian Affairs, hoped that the Public Works Administration might allocate funds for the work. The tribe also grew agitated, but the Interior Department was at an impasse. Interior Secretary Harold L. Ickes reasoned that the Federal Power Act did not authorize the "granting of an indefinite extension of the fixed time for construction," particularly when the company had abandoned the project. The Flathead informed Ickes that the postponement and loss of royalties was "prejudicial" to the tribe. Moreover, with full knowledge of depression conditions, Montana Power had signed the contract requiring the payment of a fixed rental independent of the output of the power site and its profits. The tribe could "not be expected now to assume the burdens of the licensee's financial distress." Finally, the company rejected the conditions of extension obliging it to pay the tribe and irrigation project for losses. In late 1934, Ickes recommended cancellation of the license or filing suit against Montana Power for damages, while Senator Burton Wheeler proposed legislation for $5 million in Public Works funding to build the project.[39]

Nevertheless, the Interior Department made little progress in 1935. In exasperation, Ickes turned the case over to the U.S. Attorney General. To his consternation, the Attorney General recommended a five-year extension to complete the power site construction, "a waiver of the substantial damages accruing in favor of the Flathead Indians by reason of the past default," and a reduction of the sum paid to the tribe during the five-year period from $420,000 to $60,000, with further reductions in successive years. Ickes argued that the modifications tended "toward monopoly and [were] inconsistent with the spirit, if not the letter, of the Federal Water Power Act." The proposal deferred the rights of the Flathead and was contrary to good public policy. The situation required "prompt, firm, decisive action," not the prevarication that favored Montana Power. Ickes contended that the company had been "encouraged to propose successively worse settlements by the failure of the Government thus far to take any legal action to secure redress to the Flathead Indians." In the spring of 1936, Solicitor of the

Interior Nathan R. Margold negotiated an agreement with Montana and Rocky Mountain Power to complete the work, but Frank Kerr, president of the company, failed to show up at the appointment to close the deal. In June, the Interior Department issued a letter "designed to serve as a last and official warning that action must be taken immediately." Finally, Montana Power agreed to a new contract. It required immediate commencement of work, preference rights for employing Indians, annual rental charges amounting to $929,000 between 1936 and 1955, four percent interest on deferred payments, and damages of $500 a day for delay of completion beyond May 23, 1939. Commissioner Collier concluded that tribal interests were "exhaustively protected."[40]

By the summer of 1937, the residents of the Flathead Reservation began to see substantial results from the new power deal. Since the company resumed the work the previous year, the number of users of electric service jumped by one thousand and the "growth of the project" more than doubled since commencement in 1931. By 1940, the power sites delivered electricity to over 2,600 customers. In addition, the Flathead Irrigation Project received 15,000 horsepower for pumping, other project uses, and for resale to reimburse costs of irrigation construction. Montana Power had completed two plants by June of 1940, generating over $830,000 in total revenue.[41]

Nonetheless, the Flathead power project could not escape its troubled past. Though disputes did not erupt until 1942, two questions arose: the cost of power and whether Montana Power had a valid claim for payment on power between 1934 and 1942. According to the Indian Office, the first ten thousand horsepower delivered to the irrigation project came at a rate of one cent per kilowatt hour and all electricity over that amount had a charge of two and one half cents. The company argued that payment should be based on a monthly peak demand—a figure always over 10,000 horsepower—thus determining the cost of electricity based on the higher amount. The Federal Power Commission, as arbitrator in the matter, sided with the Indian Office.

The original contract with Montana Power required the completion of three power plants generating 150,000 horsepower. After the company's default, the amended 1936 contract for power development called for at least two plants with a capacity of 154,000 horsepower. The new agreement required the delivery of electricity as soon as any plant could be placed in commercial operation, which occurred in June of 1938. However between 1934 and 1942 the irrigation project did not have a transmission line and the company provided power via a temporary one. The amended contract contained a provision intended to "exact a penalty" for the company's failure to provide service beginning on May 23, 1934. The provision secured credit for the government on behalf of the Flathead Project for all sums paid in

Left sitting, Sakalí Finley.

excess of one cent per kilowatt hour for energy used by the project after June 1, 1934. In short, the amendment provided a "retroactive effect" to reduce to one cent the two and one-half cent rate proposed by the original contract for energy delivered during construction.[42]

Despite the requirements of the contract, and the ruling of the power commission, Montana Power refused to meet its obligations. Instead, it brashly reported a "willingness" to settle the claim for all power at the two and one-half cent rate. Indian Office administrators became fed up with the conflicts plaguing the project and agreed to pay the higher rate, with the understanding that the one-cent rate would apply to future power costs. The BIA issued almost $19,000 for power rental for ninety-two months between 1934 and 1942. By the end of World War II the dispute went into remission. Anaconda Copper became the largest consumer of power generated on the Flathead Reservation, but many small towns also "enjoyed" electrical service. In addition, many farm homes at Flathead, including Indian households, received electricity at bargain prices. Finally, the government, as guardian of the tribe, deposited tribal royalties from power into the U.S. Treasury.[43]

When Montana Power completed the third power plant on the Flathead Reservation in 1954, the tribe reiterated complaints about the amount the company owed them. In the ensuing few years, the company disregarded any ethical obligation to pay more royalties for the increased amount of power generated on tribal lands and rivers. John W. Cragun, attorney for the tribe, argued that the operation of the new power site without a revised license amounted to a federal felony. He declared, "I have seldom known greater arrogance than that which prompted [the] Montana Power Company…to go ahead and operate beyond the law, and excusing it on the ground that they would make retroactive payments to the Tribe as if it were a lawful operation." The amended license of 1936 stipulated regulations for company debts owed the tribe for the operation of two plants, but the third had an additional market value of $90,000. Finally, in September of 1958, Montana Power and the Flathead tribe settled the dispute. The company purportedly agreed to pay the Indians an extra $50,000, increasing the annual payment to the Flathead to $225,000. In return, the tribe would honor the fifty-year license with the company.[44]

On left, Sakalí Finley.

Questions remained about the power utilized via the third plant. The Flathead tribe demanded the additional $50,000, but Montana Power contended that the Federal Power Commission gave it authority to construct the third plant "without prejudice"—or changes—to the contract for power. In short, the company argued that the agreement for hydroelectric development set a general, annual charge for all power and did not discriminate between the number of plants. The tribal council requested an investigation by the Interior Department, hoping that it would invalidate Montana Power's claim that it did not owe them a higher payment. In a report issued by the tribe, "Background of the Problem of the Indians of the Flathead Reservation and Their Dam Sites," they described their point of view: "The white man feels strongly that he can make better use of the Indian [natural] resources than can the Indian. Therefore he proposes to seize it for his own." The Flathead contended that in Montana Power's pursuit to gain control of all tribal energy resources, it merely satisfied the "minimum requirements of the law of eminent domain" even though it would cost less to pay royalties to them. The company's quest to monopolize power in Montana overrode any consideration for tribal wishes. What Montana Power failed to realize, the Flathead explained, was that the Indians did "not oppose full development of those resources," but merely asked "to share in the development."[45]

The Flathead report on the power dispute was a preeminent example of tribal sovereignty and self-government. When congress passed the Indian Reorganization Act of 1934 (IRA), the Flathead reorganized their tribal council and wrote a constitution that outlined their vision of the management of natural resources. As the Flathead put it, the "tribe constitute[s] a government," not just because the Hellgate Treaty of 1855 guaranteed that right, but because the IRA and tribal constitution provided them with "current executive, legislative, and judicial functions." In the late 1950s, the U.S. Army Corps of Engineers proposed the Knowles-Paradise Dam near the Flathead Reservation. Even though it would "flood out" two dam-power sites on the reservation scheduled for development by Montana Power, the corps did not consult the tribe.[46]

With the consummation of the Paradise plans, the tribal council reported, "will go our hopes and plans for a tribal income which, from Kerr Dam, has helped many of our people get on their feet and become some of the most progressive and accomplished Indian people anywhere.... The shock to the Indian economy will be profound." The corps' dam would impair hunting and fishing rights, tribal Christmas-tree operations, other forestry enterprises, and tribal grazing. The legislation for Paradise proposed a single cash payment to compensate the tribe for its losses, but the Flathead claimed it "would result in a boom (while the money lasts) and bust (when the Indian people try to go on relief, which is largely withheld from them in Montana)." Instead, the tribe wanted royalties, as with the Kerr Dam power sites, for "continuing income for the betterment of our people." The Flathead Tribal Council concluded, "We feel that since the Flathead people have by treaty maintained the exploitable values in these dam sites, it is only just that they—and not the United States by grabbing the Indian property away from them—should realize the tremendous increment in value which it is known will accrue from the head developed on tribal lands."[47]

The arguments about the Paradise proposal directly related to the controversy about the third power plant on the Flathead Reservation. In 1961, the Flathead tribe intervened in the case of *The Montana Power Company v. The Federal Power Commission*. The company had filed suit to prevent the federal government from instituting additional charges for the third plant. Federal Power Commission regulations and the license to Montana Power for developing electricity at Flathead provided that further development—beyond the first power site—must "result in a corresponding increase of Indian rental based upon the increased earning power of site No. 1." The power commission determined that the "additional exploitation of the tribal dam site required payment of $50,000 a year in annual charges for the benefit of the Tribes." However, the Interior Secretary had the final say in tribal natural resource matters and he "determined that $63,375 was more appropriate." The power commission consented, but Montana Power refused to pay that amount. In 1961, largely due to the efforts of the tribal report and protests, the court decided in favor of the Indians, raising their annual income to over $250,000.[48]

Indians' views of Flathead hyrdroelectric development are certainly debatable. As historian Jaako Puisto has pointed out, not all Flathead wanted to exploit the dam and power sites. Puisto suggests that the character Bull, in D'Arcy McNickle's *Wind From An Enemy Sky*, represented "many Indians' true feelings about the [Kerr] Dam." In an act of defiance, Bull shot at the dam, declaring, "They can't stop the water.... The water was there when the world began. What kind of fool would want to stop it!" Undoubtedly, Bull served as a good symbol of the controversy over power among the Flathead, Montana Power, and federal officials. Some Flathead would have agreed with Bull, but many more wanted the electricity and income. More important than his declaration about the dam, another of Bull's poignant statements foreshadowed the future of power utilization. Bull's grandson, Antoine, related a story of the disciplinarian at his boarding school inflating himself into a "big man" by using his leather belt on the students. The government and corporate interests had a power similar to the "man with a whip in his hand." Bull warned his grandson not to forget his actions at the dam, asking him to remember that the "white man makes us forget our holy places. He makes us small." The fifty-year lease awarded to the Montana Power Company guaranteed a set income for the tribe. Despite the escalating value of electrical power, the inequitable contract minimized the role of the Flathead Indians.[49]

In 1981, nearly fifty years after the contract let to Montana Power, the Flathead came to a new crossroads in the use of waterpower. The tribe's work in natural resources—forestry, minerals, water, wildlife, and hydropower—proved that they had learned the harsh lessons of federal policy and gained an "expertise and ambition" in managing the tribal environment. In 1981, they petitioned the federal government for control of their hydroelectric power. When Montana Power's fifty-year license expired in 1985, the tribal council brokered a new deal. They estimated the company's annual net profit from power developed at Flathead between $12 and $14 million. The tribe negotiated a new thirty-year contract with Montana Power with an

Kerr Dam dedication. Second from left, Mathias. Fourth from left, Chief Martin Charlo. Fifth from left, Chief Koostahtah. Sixth from left, Victor Vanderburg. Seventh from left, Frank Kerr.

annual payment of $9 million to the Indians. The Flathead wisely inserted a clause providing for adjustment of the payment based on inflation. In 2015, the Flathead tribe assumed full control and operation of their power sites.[50]

The final agreement, as one historian noted, allowed the Flathead "to dismiss assertions that economic development has to be defined in terms of resource exploitation." It seemed that the Flathead heeded Bull's warning. They recalled the 1930s and the "corrupting, blackmailing, and unscrupulous influence" of Montana Power. They remembered that the Federal Power Commission, War Department, and Indian Office had favored Montana Power, "perpetuating the dog-in-the-manger monopoly advantages" and "serfdom" of the tribe to the company.[51] Terming hydroelectric development at Flathead as the "Indian Muscle Shoals" aptly characterized the animus, conflict, and vast potential of the power project. Both the eastern Muscle Shoals and power development at the Flathead Reservation revealed that federal involvement in natural resource utilization came with benefits and costs. Many federal officials served as caretakers of Indian interests, but bureaucracy often limited good intentions. More importantly, the battle over Flathead power emphatically illustrated that tribal sovereignty and self-determination surpassed what federal officials believed was in the "best interest" of the Flathead Indians.

Kerr Dam dedication. Second from left, Chief Martin Charlo.
Third from left, Chief Koostahtah.

Kerr Dam dedication. L to R: unknown, Michel, Little Martin,
Snayaqn Quequesah, Alec Beaverhead.

# Afterword

This book is an excerpt from my doctoral dissertation examining federal natural resource and Native American policy related to the Flathead, Blackfeet, and Fort Peck Reservations from the late nineteenth through the middle twentieth century. Similar to the dissertation, this study reflects how Native Americans on the Flathead Reservation asserted their sovereignty and cultural values to influence the decisions made by non-Indian officials about Indian natural resource management issues. Bluntly, this was not an easy, nor equitable process. Nonetheless, the Salish, Kootenai, and Pend d'Oreille peoples did exert strong influence on the policies implemented by federal managers on the reservation.

The control that so many sought to assert on the Flatheads' daily lives and future was roundly met with what the tribes themselves thought was the best path for their people. There were exceptions, of course but many federal policy-makers and officials believed their ideas for the Indians' future superseded what the Indians themselves believed. Many thought that Indians would only persist by becoming carbon copies of non-Indians, and only by being aided by governmental oversight and assistance. And yet, as BIA Commissioner John Collier foreshadowed in 1933, "It is interesting to reflect on the reverses brought by time." While federal assistance, often in the cloak of superiority, did provide assistance to the Flathead Reservation tribes, the tribes' determination and ingenuity paved the way to a successful economy, environmental integrity, and a thriving community.

The story of the Confederated Salish and Kootenai Tribes (CSKT) is one of persistence, of commitment to cultural values, of a deep knowledge and connection to the land, wildlife, and natural resources. This tenacity is proven no better than by what we witness on the Flathead Reservation today. In 1979, the CSKT set aside nearly 90,000 acres to establish the Mission Mountain Wilderness, providing habitat for a wealth of wildlife including grizzly and black bears, mountain goats, deer, lynx and other species. After eighty years, the tribes wrested control of their power sites from corporate interests. Between the 1930s and today, the CSKT have built one of the most successful and recognized natural resource programs in the nation, managing habitat for hundreds of wildlife species. S & K Technologies, a tribally-owned and operated enterprise, employs hundreds of people, providing aerospace, engineering, technology, and other services to customers around the world. In the mid-1990s, the tribes assumed the lead from the federal government for the management of the nearly 500,000 acres of forested land on the reservation. These represent only a few of the many examples of how the CSKT have exerted their sovereignty, ecological and cultural expertise, and entrepreneurship.

This case study is indicative of the history and evolution of 20th century American Indian policy. It is representative of the conflict between Indian and non-Indian interests over Indian resources. And yet, the CSKT are unique in the power and control they have exerted. Certainly, many tribes have not been able to exercise the same amount of authority over their land and resources. The federal government continues to play a large role in Indian communities. Nonetheless, the history of the Confederated Salish and Kootenai Tribes represents a model for other tribes, an example of the true intent of self-determination.

On a final note, I would like to thank the Confederated Salish and Kootenai Tribes for the honor of presenting this history, as well as the Salish and Kootenai College Press, particularly Bob Bigart, for the extreme patience and expertise in preparing this manuscript for publication.

                                                            Garrit Voggesser.

# Notes

**Abbreviations Used in Notes**

ADR – A. D. Rogers Collection. Accession Number 1935. American Heritage Center, University of Wyoming, Laramie, Wyoming.

APDP – Arthur Powell Davis Papers. Accession Number 1366. American Heritage Center, University of Wyoming, Laramie, Wyoming.

ARCIA – Annual Report of the Commissioner of Indian Affairs and Report of the Commissioner of Indian Affairs to the Secretary of the Interior. Washington, D.C.: Government Printing Office.

ARDI – Annual Report of the Department of the Interior. Washington, D.C.: Government Printing Office.

ARSI – Annual Report of the Secretary of the Interior. Washington, D.C.: Government Printing Office.

BKW – Burton K. Wheeler Papers. Manuscript Collection 34. Montana Historical Society Archives, Helena, Montana.

CTM – Charles T. Main Collection. Accession Number 3309. American Heritage Center, University of Wyoming, Laramie, Wyoming.

EOF – E. O. Fuller Collection. Accession Number 80. American Heritage Center, University of Wyoming, Laramie, Wyoming.

FHN – Frederick H. Newell Collection. Accession Number 2068. American Heritage Center, University of Wyoming, Laramie, Wyoming.

GHE – George Henry Ellis Collection. Accession Number 2219. American Heritage Center, University of Wyoming, Laramie, Wyoming.

GHH – Gilbert H. Hogue Collection. Accession Number 2700. American Heritage Center, University of Wyoming, Laramie, Wyoming.

JMD – Joseph M. Dixon Papers. Collection 55. University of Montana, K. Ross Toole Archives, Missoula, Montana.

MGO – Montana Governor's Office: Montana Indian Historical Jurisdiction Study. Manuscript Collection 266. Montana Historical Society Archives, Helena, Montana.

MGP – Montana Governor's Papers. Manuscript Collection 35. Montana Historical Society Archives, Helena, Montana.

MPC – Montana Power Company Predecessor Company Records. Manuscript Collection 268. Montana Historical Society Archives, Helena, Montana.

Record Group 48 (RG 48). Records of the Department of the Interior. National Archives, College Park, Maryland.

   OS CCF – Office of the Secretary. Central Classified Files, 1907-1936.

Record Group 75 (RG 75). Records of the Bureau of Indian Affairs, National Archives, Denver, Colorado.

   BAO FP – Billings Area Office, Flathead Irrigation Project Subject Files, 1906-1965, Accession # 8NS-075-97-287.

   BAO FRM – Billings Area Office, Forest and Range Management Subject Files, 1930-1954, Accession # 8NS-075-97-302.

   BAO GC – Billings Area Office, Grazing Case and Subject Files, 1931-1959, Accession # 8NS-075-97-263.

   BAO MIA – Billings Area Office, Mixed Irrigation Administration and Program Files, 1916-1957, Accession # 8NS-075-97-300.

   FIP GS – Flathead Agency, Flathead Irrigation Project, General Subject Correspondence, 1908-1945, Accession # 8NS-075-97-224.

Record Group 75 (RG 75). Records of the Bureau of Indian Affairs, National Archives, Washington, D.C.

   CCF – Central Classified Files, General Service, 1907-1939.

   CCC – Civilian Conservation Corps – Indian Division, General Records, 1933-44, Flathead.

CCFF – Central Classified Files, Flathead, 1907-1939.

ID GC – Irrigation Division, General Correspondence, Entry # 653.

NAmf M1011-42 – U.S. Department of the Interior, Bureau of Indian Affairs, "Superintendents' Annual Narrative and Statistical Reports, 1907-1938," National Archives Microfilm Publication, M1011, reel 42, "Flathead, 1910-1923."

NAmf M1011-43 – U.S. Department of the Interior, Bureau of Indian Affairs, "Superintendents' Annual Narrative and Statistical Reports, 1907-1938," National Archives Microfilm Publication, M1011, reel 43, "Flathead, 1924-1935."

NAmf M1070 – U.S Department of the Interior, Bureau of Indian Affairs, "Reports of Inspection of the Field Jurisdictions of the Office of Indian Affairs, 1873-1900," National Archives Microfilm Publication, M1070, reel 11, Flathead Agency, July 10, 1883-September 12, 1900.

NAmf M1121-9 – U.S. Department of the Interior, Bureau of Indian Affairs, "Procedural Issuances: Orders and Circulars, 1854-1955," National Archives Microfilm Publication, M1121, reel 9, Numbered Circulars, 160-599, July 8, 1907-January 18, 1912.

NAmf M1121-12 – U.S. Department of the Interior, Bureau of Indian Affairs, "Procedural Issuances: Orders and Circulars, 1854-1955," National Archives Microfilm Publication, M1121, reel 12, Numbered Circulars, 1401-1900, March 5, 1918-June 30, 1923.

NAmf M1121-13 – U.S. Department of the Interior, Bureau of Indian Affairs, "Procedural Issuances: Orders and Circulars, 1854-1955," National Archives Microfilm Publication, M1121, reel 13, Numbered Circulars, 1901-2500, July 5, 1923-October 3, 1928.

NAmf M1121-14 – U.S. Department of the Interior, Bureau of Indian Affairs, "Procedural Issuances: Orders and Circulars, 1854-1955," National Archives Microfilm Publication, M1121, reel 14, Numbered Circulars, 2501-3000, October 6, 1928-June 20, 1934.

SC – Special Cases, Entry # 190.

Record Group 115 (RG 115). Records of the Bureau of Reclamation, National Archives, Denver, Colorado.

GAF – General Administrative Files, 1902-1919, Entry 3.

GPF – General Project Files, 1902-1919, Entry 3.

PF – Project Files, 1919-1929.

PF FP – Project Files, 1919-1929, Flathead Project.

RP – *The Ronan Pioneer* (Ronan, Mont.).

RWL – Rolland Wayne Lincoln Collection. Accession Number 2201. American Heritage Center, University of Wyoming, Laramie, Wyoming.

Survey of Conditions, Part 10 – U.S. Senate, *Survey of Conditions of the Indians of the United States, Part 10, "Flathead Reservation, Mont,"* Hearings Before a Subcommittee of the Committee on Indian Affairs, 71st Cong., 2d sess. (Washington, D.C.: GPO, 1930).

## Preface

1. Robert Bigart and Clarence Woodcock, eds., *In the Name of the Salish & Kootenai Nation: The 1855 Hell Gate Treaty and the Origin of the Flathead Indian Reservation* (Pablo, Mont.: Salish Kootenai College Press, 1996), pp. 10-11.

2. Peter Ronan, *"A Great Many of Us Have Good Farms": Agent Peter Ronan Reports on the Flathead Indian Reservation, 1877-1887*, ed. Robert Bigart (Pablo, Mont.: Salish Kootenai College Press, 2014), pp. 360-361.

3. Arthur M. Tinker to Secretary of the Interior, Sept. 20, 1903, Interior Department Inspection Reports, RG 48, National Archives, Washington, D.C.

4. Confederated Salish and Kootenai Tribes v. United States, U.S. Court of Claims Docket 50233, paragraph 10, decision Jan. 22, 1971.

5. Burton M. Smith, "The Politics of Allotment: The Flathead Indian Reservation as a Test Case," *Pacific Northwest Quarterly*, vol. 70, no. 3 (July 1979), pp. 131-140. Reprinted as Burton M. Smith, *The Politics of Allotment on the Flathead Indian Reservation* (Pablo, Mont.: Salish Kootenai College Press, 1995).

6. *U.S. Statutes at Large*, vol. 33, pt. 1 (1903-1905), pp. 302-306.

7. Ronald Lloyd Trosper, "The Economic Impact of the Allotment Policy on the Flathead Indian Reservation," unpublished Ph.D. dissertation, Harvard University, Cambridge, Mass., 1974, pp. 347-348.

8. *U.S. Statutes at Large*, vol. 35 (1907-1909), p. 450.

9. *U.S. Statutes at Large*, vol. 39, pt. 1 (1915-1917), p. 141.

10. *U.S. Statutes at Large*, vol. 62, pt. 1 (1948), pp. 269-273.

11. U.S. Bureau of Indian Affairs, *Flathead Project Montana: Plan for Completion* (Billings, Mont. U.S. Bureau of Indian Affairs, 1962).

## Chapter 1

1. F. H. Newell, "Irrigation of Indian Lands," An Address by F. H. Newell, former Chief, U. S. Reclamation Service, at Lake Mohonk Conference on the Indian, Mohonk Lake, New York, October 15, 1929, Box 1435, "5-6, Insurance Irrigation," Folder, "Indian Office, General, Irrigation. August 2, 1919-April 7, 1930," OS CCF.

2. Allan G. Bogue, "An Agricultural Empire," in Clyde Milner, et al, ed., *The Oxford History of the American West* (New York: Oxford University Press, 1994), 275-314.

3. Toole explains honyockers: "The origin of the word honyocker is obscure. It was apparently an offshoot of the word Hunyak, meaning an immigrant from Central Europe. It was a term of derision applied to all 'outlanders.'" K. Ross Toole, *Montana: An Uncommon Land* (Norman: University of Oklahoma Press, 1959), and K. Ross Toole, *Twentieth-Century Montana: A State of Extremes* (Norman: University of Oklahoma Press, 1972); S.T. Harding. "Irrigation Development in Montana," Bulletin No. 103, Bozeman: Montana Agriculture Experiment Station (January, 1915): 214.

4. *Flathead Project, Montana: Annual Project History, 1910*, vol. 1, RG 115, 6-8; "Synopsis of Report On Inspection of Flathead Agency by Inspector Henry Ward," November 17, 1884, "Report on Inspection of Flathead Agency by Inspector Robert Gardener," January 30, 1885, and "Synopsis of Report on Inspection of Flathead Agency by Inspector William W. Junkin," September 13, 1889, NAmf M1070.

5. ARSI 1886, 69; ARSI 1887, 28.

6. ARCIA in ARSI 1886, 96-97; "Synopsis of Report on Inspection of Flathead Agency by Inspector James Cisney," February 28, 1890, NAmf M1070.

7. "Synopsis of Report on Inspection of Flathead Agency by Inspector James Cisney," February 28, 1890, "Report on Inspection of Flathead Agency by Inspector James Cisney," February 28, 1890, and "Synopsis of Report on Inspection of Flathead Agency by Inspector Robert Gardener," August 7, 1890, NAmf M1070.; ARSI 1889, 51st Cong., 1st sess., Vol. I, H. ex. doc. 1, part 5, Serial 2724 (Washington: GPO, 1890), CXII-CXIII.

8. ARSI 1890, X-XIII; ARCIA 1890, CI.

9. "Report on Inspection of Flathead Agency by Inspector Berry H. Miller," December 15, 1891 and "Report on Inspection of Flathead Agency by Inspector McCormick," December 2, 1893, NAmf M1070; ARCIA 1891, 275-76; ARCIA in ARSI 1892, vol. 2, 292; ARCIA in ARSI 1892-93, 92.

10. ARCIA 1893, 184-85; ARCIA 1894, 174.

11. Recall that Ronan's original Jocko River ditch was only six miles in length. And, by 1896, the addition of another ditch on the east side of Jocko added only another 4 miles.

12. "Report on Inspection of Flathead Agency by Inspector McCormick," February 18, 1895 and "Report on Inspection of Flathead Agency by Inspector C. C. Duncan," October 10, 1896, NAmf M1070; ARCIA 1895, 191; ARCIA 1896, 185.

13. Inspector W. J. McConnell to the Secretary of the Interior, August 31, 1897 and "Report of Inspector McConnell to cession by Flathead Indians of a portion of their reservation, with recommendations thereon," Acting Commissioner of Indian Affairs Thomas Smith to the Secretary of the Interior, September 17, 1897, NAmf M1070.

14. Inspector W. J. McConnell to the Secretary of the Interior, August 31, 1897; Thomas Smith, Acting Commissioner of Indian Affairs, to the Secretary of the Interior, September 17, 1897, and Cyrus Beede to Ethan Allen Hitchcock, Secretary of the Interior, July 31, 1899, NAmf M1070, Roll 11, "Flathead Agency, July 10, 1883-September 12, 1900"; "Report of Flathead Agency," in ARCIA 1897, 167; ARSI 1904 in ARDI 1904, 40; "Report of Flathead Agency," in ARCIA 1899, 219-20.

15. The exactness of BIA statistics is questionable. Variations exist between different reports, data is sometimes incomplete, and personal motivations certainly played a role. ARCIA 1890, 470-73; ARCIA 1899, 219-20; ARCIA 1900, 662-65; W. H. Smead, Flathead Agent, to the Commissioner of Indian Affairs, February 27, 1900, SC.

16. ARCIA 1900, 268; W. H. Smead to the Commissioner of Indian Affairs, February 27, 1900.

17. Of course, Newell was self-interested. Before the creation of the Reclamation Service in 1902, Newell headed the U.S. Geological Survey's Hydrographic Branch, which was vying with the U.S. Army Corps of Engineers for control of federal reclamation projects. F. H. Newell, "Water Supply for Indian Reservations," in *Annual Report of the Board of Indian Commissioners, 1900* (Washington, D.C.: GPO, 1901), 37-38; Donald J. Pisani, *To Reclaim A Divided West: Water, Law, and Public Policy, 1848-1902* (Albuquerque: University of New Mexico Press, 1992), 302.

18. "Report of Agent for Flathead Agency," ARCIA 1904, 229-30; RG 115, *Flathead Project, Montana: Annual Project History, 1910*, vol. 1, 10.

19. ARSI 1905 in ARDI 1905, 57-8; ARCIA 1906, 82-4; ARCIA 1907, 54-6; *Flathead Project, Montana: Annual Project History, 1910*, vol. 1, 13; ARSI 1907 in ARDI 1907, 19.

20. Philip P. Wells, Law Officer, U.S. Forest Service, "Memorandum for Mr. Woodruff," February 1, 1908, and Joseph M. Dixon, Senate Committee on the Conservation of National Resources, to R. A. Ballinger, Secretary of the Interior, October 24, 1909, Box 1193, "5-1, Flathead P-T," Folder, "Indian Office, Flathead, Timber. January 27, 1905-March 21, 1913," OS CCF; Commissioner of Indian Affairs to Joseph T. Robinson, Chairman, Joint Commission to Investigate Indian Affairs, U.S. Senate, n.d. (ca. January, 1914), Box 36, Folder, "Flathead Agency Files, 1910-1916," ID GC; C. H. Fitch, Acting Director, Reclamation Service, to H. N. Savage, Supervising Engineer, August 18, 1908, Box 262, Folder, "858. Funds, General, Flathead Project," GAF.

21. Flathead Allottees to the Secretary of the Interior, August 26, 1909, H. N. Savage, Supervising Engineer, to the Director of the Reclamation Service, October 2, 1909, Morris Bien, Acting Director of the Reclamation Service, to the Secretary of the Interior, October 29, 1909, F. H. Abbott, Acting Commissioner of Indian Affairs, to the Secretary of the Interior, November 10, 1909, and A. P. Davis, Acting Director of the Reclamation Service, to the Secretary of the Interior, November 18, 1909, Box 470, Folder, "1002. Flathead Project, Lands, General," GPF.

22. F. H. Abbott, Acting Commissioner of Indian Affairs, to the Secretary of the Interior, November 10, 1909; A. P. Davis, Acting Director of the Reclamation Service, to the Secretary of the Interior, November 18, 1909.

23. H. N. Savage, Supervising Engineer, to the Director of the Reclamation Service, December 1, 1909, Box 470, Folder, "1002. Flathead Project, Lands, General," GPF.

24. "Memorandum Regarding $300,000 appropriation for irrigation system on Flathead Indian Reservation Montana," December 15, 1910, Box 262, Folder, "858. Funds, General, Indian Projects. Thru 1911," GAF; *Ninth Annual Report of the Reclamation Service, 1909-1910* (Washington, D.C.: GPO, 1911), 144; "Changing Allotments and Resultant Consequences," RP, May 26, 1911, 1; "Unclassified and Unappraised Flathead Land," RP, June 23, 1911, 1.

25. "Appraisement and Classification of Land Asked," RP, July 28, 1911, 1; "Indian Department Policy Detrimental to Progress," RP, December 1, 1911, 1; "Senators and Representatives are Requested to Help," RP, December 8, 1911, 1-3.

26. "Senators and Representatives are Requested to Help," 1-3; "Annual Report of Fred C. Morgan on Flathead Agency, 1911," NAmf 1011-42; "Major Morgan Interviewed On Reservation Matters," RP, January 5, 1912, 1; "Senators and Representatives Are Requested to Help," RP, December 8, 1911, 1, 3, 4.

27. "Rich in Flathead Lands, Entire Family Suffers," RP, March 8, 1912, 1; Camas Hot Springs Commercial Club to Frances Warren, Secretary of the Interior, March 20, 1912, Box 1189, "5-1, Flathead I," Folder, "Indian Office, Flathead, Irrigation – General. May 16, 1907-April 28, 1924," OS CCF.

28. Acting Secretary of the Interior to Joseph M. Dixon, September 1, 1910, and Acting Secretary of the Interior to Fred C. Morgan, Flathead Superintendent, September 16, 1910, Box 1190, "5-1, Flathead I," Folder, "Indian Office, Flathead, Irrigation – Water Rights. September 1, 1910-October 4, 1915," OS CCF; W. M. Code, Memorandum, "Flathead Reservation," January 16, 1911, Box 36, "Flathead Agency Files, 1910-1916," ID GC.

29. "Give the Farmer Fair Play and Do it Now," RP, September 1, 1911, 1.

30. R. G. Valentine, Commissioner of Indian Affairs, to F. H. Newell, Director of Reclamation Service, October 3, 1911 and A. P. Davis, Acting Director, Reclamation Service, to H. N. Savage, Supervising Engineer, Reclamation Service, October 7, 1911, Box 262, Folder, "858. Funds, General, Indian Projects. Thru 1911," GAF; "Indians Want Money," RP, January 12, 1912, 1.

31. "Friends of the Flathead Will Try to Help Us," RP, April 5, 1912, 1.

32. "Prevent Issuing Patents," RP, July 19, 1912, 1; "Settlers Are Again Warned," RP, August 30, 1912, 1; "More About Timber Lands," RP, January 23, 1913, 1.

33. Frederick Newell, Director of the Reclamation Service, to F. H. Abbott, Acting Commissioner of Indian Affairs, February 8, 1913 and Frederick Newell to H. L. Myers, U.S. Senate, February 15, 1913, Box 263, Folder, "858. Funds, General, Indian Projects, 1912-1914," GAF; "Secretary Lane Wants Changes," RP, June 27, 1913, 1.

34. "Secretary Lane and His Party Visit Ronan," RP, August 15, 1913, 1, 4; "Will Provide Means For Indians To Farm," RP, August 22, 1913, 1; "Disappointed," RP, August 22, 1913, 2.

35. "Surplus of Farm Lands; A Scarcity of Farmers," RP, November 14, 1913, 1; ARSI 1914 in ARDI 1914, 12.

36. Cato Sells, Commissioner of Indian Affairs, to the Secretary of the Interior, August 27, 1914, Box 1193, "5-1, Flathead, P-T," Folder, "Indian Office, Flathead, Timber. August 10, 1914-November 29, 1924," OS CCF; Secretary of the Interior to the Attorney General, July 12, 1911, Box 1194, "5-1, Flathead, T-W," Folder, "Indian Office, Flathead, Trespass – General," OS CCF.

37. These "squatters" demanded that both lands classified for timber and reservoir sites be thrown open immediately.

38. M. L. Dorr, "A Report to the Secretary of the Interior on the Flathead Indian Reservation," June 2, 1914, Box 1189, "5-1, Flathead I," no folder (loose in box), OS CCF; William H. Ketcham, *Report Upon the Conditions On the Flathead Reservation* (Washington, D.C.: Board of Indian Commissioners, 1915), 21-6.

39. Ketcham, 25-28.

40. Commissioner of Indian Affairs to Joseph T. Robinson, Chairman, Joint Commission to Investigate Indian Affairs, U.S. Senate, n.d. [ca. January, 1914] and Chief Engineer, Indian Irrigation Service, Memorandum, "Laws Pertaining to Irrigation on the Flathead Reservation," January 29, 1914, Box 36, "Flathead Agency Files, 1910-1916," ID GC.

41. In *Lone Wolf v. Hitchcock* (1903), the Supreme Court asserted the federal government's authority to act without Indian consent; theoretically, federal officials would act in the best interests of Indians and their resources. 187 U.S. 553-68.

42. F. H. Abbott, Secretary, Board of Indian Commissioners. "Brief on Indian Irrigation," 1915, Box 3, ID GC; Cato Sells, Commissioner of Indian Affairs to the Secretary of the Interior, March 13, 1914, Box 1436, Folder, "Indian Office, General, Irrigation. November 11, 1912-October 17, 1917," OS CCF.

43. This figure indicated a steady increase in farming by Indians. In 1911, Indians cultivated only 20,000 acres.

44. Frederick Newell, Director of the Reclamation Service to H.N. Savage, Supervising Engineer, August 8, 1914, Box 263, Folder, "858. Funds, General, Indian Projects, 1912-1914," GAF; "Annual Report of Fred C. Morgan on Flathead Agency, 1914," NAmf M1011-42; Ketcham, *Report Upon the Conditions on the Flathead Reservation*, 29; ARCIA 1915, 121, 130-31, 180; "Why Indian Bill Failed to Pass," RP, March 12, 1915, 1.

45. The methods of controlling funding and procuring reimbursement for costs of irrigation on the Indian Irrigation Projects led to intense battles between Davis and Lane. "Director Newell Says 20 Years," RP, October 9, 1914, 1; Cato Sells, Commissioner of Indian Affairs, to W. A. Ryan, Comptroller of the Reclamation Service, November 5, 1914, Box 263, Folder, "858. Funds, General, Indian Projects, 1912-1914," GAF; "Changes of Force," July 27, 1915, Box 13, Folder 6, APDP.

46. In the past, funds appropriated to each bureau, if not used up, rolled over and remained available for the next year. Using an obscure 1912 act, the Treasury Department in 1914 decided that interpretation of the use of funds no longer applied. This meant, for example, that the unexpended balance of $187,000 for the Flathead in 1914 did not roll over to 1915, entailing an entire cessation of work on the irrigation project. H. P. Seidemann, Acting Comptroller, "Memorandum for Mr. Ryan," December 10, 1914, Morris Bien, Chief Counsel, Reclamation Service, "Memorandum for Reclamation Commission," December 12, 1914, and Reclamation Commission to the Commissioner of Indian Affairs, December 14, 1914, Box 263, Folder, "858. Funds, General, Indian Projects, 1912-1914," GAF.

47. Much of Reclamation's debt was incurred by supplying equipment and materials for irrigation work prior to being reimbursed by the Indian Office via tribal funds from the sale of surplus lands. A. P. Davis, Director of the Reclamation Service, to the Secretary of the Interior, April 28, 1915 and Cato Sells, Commissioner of Indian Affairs, to the Secretary of the Interior, May 24, 1915, Box 263, Folder. "858. Funds, General, Indian Projects, 1915," GAF.

48. Senator H. L. Meyers to Franklin K. Lane, Secretary of the Interior, September 3, 1915 and Senator H. L. Meyers to Franklin K. Lane, September 16, 1915, Box 1189, "5-1, Flathead I," Folder, "Indian Office, Flathead, Irrigation – Appropriations," OS CCF; "Annual Report of Fred C. Morgan on Flathead Agency, 1916," NAmf M1011-42; ARCIA 1915, 51; ARCIA 1916, 46-47.

49. "No Reclamation Data Will Be Given Settlers," RP, February 16, 1912, 1; "Annual Report of Fred C. Morgan on Flathead Agency, 1915," NAmf M1011-42.

50. "Indian Chiefs Off To Capital," RP, January 12, 1917, 1; "Indians Charge Extravagance," RP, February 23, 1917, 1; "Annual Report of Fred C. Morgan on Flathead Agency, 1916" and "Annual Report of Theodore Sharp on Flathead Agency, 1917," NAmf M1011-42; ARCIA 1916, 113, 561.

51. ARCIA 1916, 166-67; "Indians Charge Extravagance," 1; "Flathead Project-Montana: Report On Operation & Maintenance, Year 1917," Box 5, GHH.

52. "Flathead Fight For $750,000 Appropriation," RP, February 15, 1918, 1; "$375,000 for Work on Flathead Project," RP, April 12, 1918, 1; "Annual Report of Theodore Sharp on Flathead Agency, 1918," NAmf M1011-42.

53. C. J. Moody to Andrew D. Robinson, November 16, 1953, Box 3, Folder, "Indian Irrigation Book 1," ADR; G. L. Sperry to Andrew D. Rodgers, July 1, 1957, Box 2, Folder, "Indian Irrigation Book 1," ADR.

54. E. B. Meritt, Assistant Commissioner, to Theodore Sharp, Flathead Superintendent, July 12, 1919, Box 12, Folder 5, "Flathead,1911-1933," MGO.

55. "Report of Commission on Water Rights, Vol. 1," December 10, 1919, Box 523, Folder, "032. Flathead Project, Settlement of Water Rights, Report Dated 12-10-19 Of Com. On Water Rights," PF. Emphasis in original.

56. C. J. Moody, Flathead Project Manager, to Willis J. Egleston, District Counsel, Reclamation Service, April 29, 1921, Box 524, Folder, "032. Flathead Project, Settlement of Water Rights (A to Z)," PF.

57. Willis J. Egleston, District Counsel, Reclamation Service, to Ottamar Hamele, Chief Counsel, April 30, 1921 and Willis J. Egleston to C. J. Moody, Flathead Project Manager, May 3, 1921, Box 524, Folder, "032. Flathead Project, Settlement of Water Rights (A to Z)," PF; Assistant Secretary of the Interior to the Attorney General of the United States, April 30, 1921, Box 1191, "5-1, Flathead I-L," Folder "Indian Office, Flathead, Irrigation – Water Rights. May 4, 1916-May 15, 1924," OS CCF.

58. Circular 1677, "Sale of irrigable lands," Commissioner Charles H. Burke to Superintendents, May 12, 1921, NAmf M1121-12; ARSI 1921, 9; RG 115, *Flathead Annual Project History, 1921*, vol. 29, 1.

59. C. J. Moody, Flathead Project Manager, to A. P. Davis, Director of the Reclamation Service, May 28, 1921 and E. B. Meritt, Assistant Commissioner of Indian Affairs, to A. P. Davis, June 14, 1921, Box 530, Folder, "225.01. Flathead Project, Correspondence re. Entrymen Delinquent in Payment of Water Right Charges," PF; ARSI 1921, 14-15.

60. G. L. Sperry, "The Flathead (Indian) Project," *Reclamation Record* 13:6 (June 1922), 126; C. J. Moody, Flathead Project Manager, to A. P. Davis, Director of the Reclamation Service, March 17, 1923, Box 531, Folder, "500. Flathead Project, Settlement and Colonization," PF.

61. Charles H. Burke, Commissioner of Indian Affairs, to A. P. Davis, Director of the Reclamation Service, May 4, 1923, Box 522, Folder, "032. Flathead Reservation. Settlement of Water Rights," PF.

62. Ibid.; Morris Bien, "Memorandum for Mr. Hamele," May 18, 1923, Box 522, Folder, "032. Flathead Reservation. Settlement of Water Rights," PF.

63. Donald Pisani pointed out that the Indian Office had difficulty finding a "practical way to apply the *Winters* decision, especially once allotment began." Pisani, "Uneasy Allies: The Reclamation Service and the Bureau of Indian Affairs," in *Water and the American Government: The Reclamation Bureau, National Water Policy, and the West, 1902-1935* (Berkeley: University of California Press, 2002), 162-67.

64. George A. Ward, "Memorandum for Mr. Hamele," May 21, 1923, Box 522, Folder, "032. Flathead Reservation. Settlement of Water Rights," PF; William Zimmerman, Assistant Commissioner of Indian Affairs, to W. S. Hanna, Supervising Engineer, Indian Irrigation Service, July 29, 1939, Box 7, Folder, "Water Supply, 1939," BAO FP; "Wheeler Attacks Reclamation Policy," RP, November 2, 1923, 1.

65. Recall, that it was in this period that the Reclamation Service's budget was put on an "appropriation basis," requiring that the Indian Office front the money for all supplies and materials rather than having the Reclamation Service spend its money on Indian irrigation. At the time, the Reclamation Service paid for costs of construction on the Indian projects, and then the Indian Office reimbursed the Reclamation Service. The objection to the process centered on using Reclamation Service funds intended for "white" projects to fund work on Indian reservations, even though repayment would eventually come from the Indians or congressional appropriations to the Indian Office. Pisani, "Uneasy Allies" 154-80; Frederick H. Newell, Director of the Reclamation Service, to Warren L. Fisher, Secretary of the Interior, July 11, 1911, Warren L. Fisher to the Comptroller of the Treasury, July 13, 1911, and Warren L. Fisher to the Comptroller of the Treasury, July 25, 1911, Box 1189, "5-1, Flathead I," Folder, "Indian Office, Flathead, Irrigation – Cooperation," OS CCF.

66. Frederick Newell, Director of the Reclamation Service to H. N. Savage Supervising Engineer, March 30, 1914, Box 263, Folder, "858. Funds, General, Indian Projects, 1912-1914," GAF; A. P. Davis, Director of the Reclamation Service, to the Secretary of the Interior, April 28, 1915, Box 263, Folder. "858. Funds, General, Indian Projects, 1915," GAF; A. P. Davis to the Secretary of the Interior, March 14, 1916 and Andrius A. Jones, First Assistant Secretary, to Cato Sells, Commissioner, April 10, 1916,Box 1189, "5-1, Flathead I," Folder, "Indian Office, Flathead, Irrigation – Appropriations," OS CCF.

67. "Myers, Walsh, and Evans," RP, November 13, 1914, 1; Henry L. Myers, to Montana Governor Joseph M. Dixon, November 21, 1921, Box 31, Folder 2, "Irrigation Projects," MGP; Charles H. Burke, Commissioner of Indian Affairs to Senator Thomas Walsh (Montana), December 22, 1921 and Charles H. Burke to Senator Thomas Walsh, December 22, 1921, Box 938, Folder, "38841-1920," CCF.

68. *Flathead Annual Project History, 1921*, vol. 29, RG 115 (National Archives, Denver), 61-2, 155, 159; "Annual Statistical Report, Flathead Agency, 1921," NAmf M1011-43, 42-3; Charles H. Burke, Commissioner of Indian Affairs, "Memorandum for First Assistant Secretary," April 18, 1922, Box 938, Folder, "38841-1920," CCF; W. W. Von Segen, Little Bitter Root Valley Water Users Association, to A. P. Davis, Director of the Reclamation Service, April 20, 1922, Box 529, Folder, "223.02. Flathead Project, Correspondence re. Lease of Water," PF; Morris Bien, Assistant Director of the Reclamation Service, to Harry Morris, August 4, 1922, Box 530, Folder, "225.11. Flathead Project, Payment of Construction Charges," PF.

69. "Operation of Indian Projects Transferred," *Reclamation Record* 15:2 (February 1924), 31.

70. Charles Burke, Commissioner of Indian Affairs, "Memorandum for the Secretary," December 6, 1924, Box 3, ID GC.

71. Ralph Carleton, "How One Farmer Makes Things Go," RP, May 11, 1923, 1; "Lars Beck Ranch Is Widely Advertised," RP, August 10, 1923, 1. Historian Donald Pisani also related the story of Beck, but it is useful to contrast the story of this "diligent" yeoman farmer with the more typical experiences of white farmers on the reservation. See Donald J. Pisani, "Federal Reclamation and the American West in the Twentieth Century," *Agricultural History* 77: 3 (Summer 2003): 394-95.

72. Edith Siner to the General Land Office, March 19, 1924, Box 531, Folder, "400. Flathead Project, Lands, General," PF FP; W. H. Beacom, Mayor of Missoula, to Montana Senator John M. Evans, March 25, 1924, Box 530, Folder, "225.03. Flathead Project, Correspondence re. Application of Penalties on Entrymen," PF; "Cramton Talks To Ronan," RP, August 7, 1925, 1.

73. "Annual Statistical Report, Flathead Agency, 1925," NAmf M1011-43, 31-3; "Tribal Council Ask Investigation," RP, January 23, 1925, 1; "Irrigation As Dr. Work, Sec. Of The Interior, Sees It," RP, July 3, 1925, 1.

74. "Annual Report of Charles E. Coe on Flathead Agency, 1925," NAmf M1011-43.

75. "Memorandum concerning the Flathead Irrigation Project," September 3, 1925, Box 36, "Flathead Agency Files, 1910-1916," ID GC; ARCIA 1925, 24-5; "Western Reclamation," RP, October 2, 1925, 1; "$575,000 For Flathead Pass By House Vote," RP, January 15, 1926, 1; "Flathead Appropriation Passes In Both Houses," RP, May 14, 1926, 1.

76. "Flathead Appropriation Is Held Up By Injunction," RP, October 1, 1926, 1; "Irrigation Districts Legally Organized," RP, November 5, 1926, 1; Charles H. Burke, "Reclamation of Indian Lands," *The Highway Magazine* 17 (November, 1926): 284-86, Box 940, Folder, "38841-1920," CCF; *Annual Report of the Board of Indian Commissioners, 1926* (Washington, D.C.: GPO, 1926), 28-9.

77. Circular 2432, "In re. Inclusion of Liens in All Patents and Instruments Executed Covering Irrigable Lands," Commissioner Charles H. Burke to Superintendents, April 4, 1928, NAmf M1121-13; "H. H. Frances, Floyd Mitchell, J. O. Mills, and Fred Chartier, Plaintiffs vs. C. J. Moody, and C. J. Moody as Project Manager of Flathead Reclamation Project," September 15, 1928, Box 21, Folder, "Litigation File, Moody Cases," BAO FP; "Annual Report of Charles E. Coe on Flathead Agency, 1928," NAmf M1011-43.

78. William S. Hanna, Supervising Engineer, Indian Irrigation Service, to the Commissioner of Indian Affairs, June 10, 1929, Box 940, Folder, "38841-1920," CCF; C. J. Rhoads, Commissioner of Indian Affairs, to Senator Lynn J. Frazier, Chairman, Senate Committee on Indian Affairs, December 11, 1929, Box 8, Folder 14, "Indian Affairs—Letters of Commissioner, 1929," BKW; "Annual Report of Charles E. Coe on Flathead Agency, 1929," NAmf M1011-43.

79. In 1926, Interior Secretary Hubert Work asked the Institute for Government Research to examine federal Indian policy. In 1928, the survey commission, led by Institute staff member Lewis Meriam, reported that the BIA's blanket policy for Indian farming ignored the needs and wishes of Indians. Many Indians were more interested in subsistence, rather than market agriculture, and the government needed to provide the tools, seeds, livestock and other items to give Indians a chance at success. The government asked Preston and Engle to look specifically at water policy on tribal lands.

80. Between 1867 and 1927 the government had spent nearly $36 million dollars to make 692,057 acres of Indian land "susceptible" of irrigation, while approximately 362,018, or only fifty-two percent, used water. On the projects, Indians irrigated thirty-two percent and whites controlled the remaining sixty-eight percent. White lessees irrigated thirty-one percent and white owners irrigated thirty-seven percent. The lack of overall usage—the fifty-two percent figure—revealed the faulty idealism of American views of irrigation. The Preston-Engle Report primarily focused on: the Yakima in Washington; the Blackfeet, Crow, Flathead, and Fort Peck in Montana; the Wind River in Wyoming; the Fort Hall in Idaho; Uintah in Utah; and Gila River in Arizona.

81. U.S. Senate, Subcommittee of the Committee on Indian Affairs, "Preston-Engle Report," in *Survey of Conditions of the Indians in the United States*, Part 6, 71st Cong., 2d sess. (Washington, D.C.: GPO, 1930), 2217, 2222.

82. Ibid., 2218-2221.

83. Ibid., 2221-2222, 2237, 2300.

84. Ibid., 2244, 2286, 2288, 2401-2404.

85. Ibid., 2424; "Annual Statistical Report, Flathead Agency, 1925," NAmf M1011-43, 19-22.

86. "Preston-Engle Report," 2424-2426, 2670.

87. Ibid., 2258-2260.

88. Ibid., 2670; "Annual Statistical Report, Flathead Agency, 1928," NAmf M1011-43, 17; ARSI 1928, 23-5.

89. Survey of Conditions, Part 10, 3268-3269.

90. Ibid., 3270-3271.

91. Ibid., 3299, 3309-3310, 3354.

92. Wheeler was the attorney for one of the factions in the tribe in the 1910s and 1920s before he was elected to the Senate. Survey of Conditions, Part 10, 3273-3281.

93. Ibid., 3272-3279.

94. Benjamin P. Harwood, Indian Office District Counsel, to Geraint Humphreys, Irrigation District Attorney, September 29, 1931, and Benjamin P. Harwood to Ethelbert Ward, November 3, 1931, Box 21, Folder, "Litigation File, Moody Cases," BAO FP.

95. Benjamin P. Harwood, District Counsel, to Ethelbert Ward, November 3, 1931 and William S. Post, Director of Irrigation, to the Commissioner of Indian Affairs, April 9, 1932, Box 21, Folder, "Litigation File, Moody Cases," BAO FP.

96. John F. Truesdell, Chief Field Counsel, to the Commissioner of Indian Affairs, August 2, 1933, T. A. Walters, First Assistant Secretary, to the Attorney General, October 10, 1933, Homer S. Cummings, Attorney General, to Harold L. Ickes, Secretary of the Interior, October 13, 1933, Kenneth R. L. Simmons, District Counsel, to Henry Gerharz, Flathead Irrigation Project Engineer, December 2, 1933, and Kenneth R. L. Simmons to Nathan R. Margold, Solicitor of the Interior, December 27, 1933, Box 21, Folder, "Litigation File, Moody Cases," BAO FP.

97. Kenneth R. L. Simmons, District Counsel, to Nathan R. Margold, Solicitor of the Interior, December 27, 1933, Box 21, Folder, "Litigation File, Moody Cases," BAO FP.

98. The Leavitt Act mandated that no construction assessments could be made against Indian lands as long as the lands remained in Indian ownership. However, it did not clearly extend relief for operation and maintenance charges, which might possibly be collectible from Indians who were considered "financially able" to make payments. The water rights disputes, in relation to the Leavitt Act, called into question the reasoning behind and purpose of the allotment act. If the government intended allotment to give Indians fee-patented property for them to make farms and become self-supporting, then, under current circumstances, not adjusting all irrigation charges due by Indians via the Leavitt Act effectively destroyed the value of an allotment. In short, land could not be made productive without water, and if irrigation charges prevented this, then not only Indian irrigation policy, but fifty years worth of Indian policy, were complete failures.

99. Kenneth R. L. Simmons, District Counsel, to Nathan R. Margold, Solicitor of the Interior, December 27, 1933; John F. Truesdell, Chief Field Counsel, to the Commissioner of Indian Affairs, August 2, 1933, Box 21, Folder, "Litigation File, Moody Cases," BAO FP; Henry Gerharz, Project Engineer, to W. S. Hanna, Supervising Engineer, Billings Region, November 19, 1934, Box 9, Folder, "Investigations," BAO FP; Kenneth R. L. Simmons to W. S. Hanna, January 8, 1936, Box 7, Folder 175.1, "Suits—1932 through 1942," BAO FP.

100. "Annual Report of Charles E. Coe on Flathead Agency, 1931" and "Annual Statistical Report, Flathead Agency, 1931, NAmf M1011-43, 5, 11; ARCIA 1932, 13, 18-9; "Deferment and Adjustment of Construction Charges on Indian Irrigation Projects," H.R. 2372, 72d Cong., 1st sess., serial 9493 (Washington, D.C.: GPO, 1932).

101. John Collier, Assistant Secretary, American Indian Defense Association, to Charles J. Rhoads, Commissioner, May 28, 1932, Box 1189, "5-1, Flathead I," Folder, "Indian Office, Flathead, Irrigation – General. August 11, 1930-November 18, 1936," OS CCF.

102. Charles E. Coe, Flathead Superintendent, to the Commissioner, September 21, 1933, Box 89, Folder, "18574-1933," CCC; "Temporary Relief of Water Users on Irrigation Projects On Indian Reservations," S.R. 1197, 72d Cong., 2d sess., serial 9647 (Washington, D.C.: GPO, 1933); ARSI 1933, 103; Circular 2979, "Irrigation Reorganization," Commissioner John Collier to Administrative Officers, February 12, 1934 and Circular 3068, "Work Relief Bill Appropriation," Commissioner John Collier to Superintendents, April 16, 1935, NAmf M1121-14; ARSI 1934, 110.

103. "Flathead Irrigation Project: Annual Irrigation Cost and Narrative Reports for Fiscal Year 1936," Box 13, Folder, "Flathead Annual Reports, 1936," BAO MIA; "Flathead Irrigation Project: Annual Irrigation Cost and Narrative Reports for Fiscal Year 1937," Box 13, Folder, "Flathead Annual Reports, 1937," BAO MIA; L. W. Shotwell, Flathead Superintendent, to D. E. Murphy, Director, CCC-ID, June 28, 1938, Box 90, Folder, "18574-33," CCC; L. W. Shotwell to the Commissioner, October 21, 1938, Box 88, Folder, "50830-36, Funds," CCC GR.

104. L. W. Shotwell, Flathead Superintendent, to the Commissioner, May 19, 1939, Box 90, Folder, "18574-33," CCC; Gordon MacGregor, "The Social Aspects of the Economy of the Flathead Reservation," Office of Indian Education, 1939, Box 1, BAO FP, 13-9.

105. "Memorandum: Flathead Reservation Reservoir Sites," September 12, 1940, Box 449, Folder, "29030, Flathead 1936," CCFF; Office of Indian Affairs, Irrigation Division, "Report On Conditions Found To Exist on the Flathead Irrigation Project, Montana," June 1946, Box 29, Folder, "Reports 6," EOF, 6.

106. E. O. Fuller, "Report: 1855 Land Values," September 30, 1953, Box 29, Folder, "Reports 5," EOF, 145-49, 157, 177-78, 301-02.

107. "Report On Conditions Found To Exist on the Flathead Irrigation Project, Montana," June 1946, 1-3; John W. Cragun, "Statement on Behalf of the Confederated Salish and Kootenai Tribes," October 21, 1957, Box 1, Folder, "Flathead Project," RWL.

### Chapter 2

1. "Report on Inspection of Flathead Agency by Inspector B. B. Benedict," July 10, 1883, NAmf M1070; Historical Research Associates, *Timber, Tribes, and Trust: A History of BIA Forest Management On the Flathead Indian Reservation (1855-1975)*, Prepared for the Confederated Salish and Kootenai Tribes of the Flathead Indian Reservation and the Bureau of Indian Affairs, Branch of Forestry, Flathead Agency (Dixon, Montana: Confederated Salish and Kootenai Tribes, 1977), 11.

2. "Report on Inspection of Flathead Agency by Inspector B. B. Benedict," July 10, 1883; *Timber, Tribes, and Trust*, 16-18; "Report on Inspection of Flathead Agency by Inspector W. A. Howard," December 4,1883, "Synopsis of Report on Inspection of Flathead Agency by Inspector Henry Ward," November 17, 1884, and "Report on Inspection of Flathead Agency by Inspector Robert Gardener," January 30, 1885, NAmf M1070.

3. "Report on Inspection of Flathead Agency by Inspector Robert Gardener," January 30, 1885; ARSI 1885, 463-65; Peter Ronan, *"A Great Many of Us Have Good Farms": Agent Peter Ronan Reports on the Flathead Indian Reservation, Montana, 1877-1887*, ed. Robert J. Bigart (Pablo, Montana: Salish Kootenai College Press, 2014), 339-342.

4. The Department reported 1,011 cases of depredation or timber trespass, involving timber valued at over six million dollars. By 1887, the Department had only recovered $128,642 in judgments and fines. The problems occurred throughout the West, but were particularly bad in California, Montana, and Idaho. In the latter two states, the government alleged that the Northern Pacific had taken over two million dollars worth of timber.

5. ARSI 1887, 165; "Report of the Commissioner of the General Land Office," in ARSI 1887, 327-28, 559; "Report of the Governor Preston H. Leslie of Montana," in ARSI 1887, 864.

6. U.S. Department of Agriculture, Forestry Division, *Report On the Relation of Railroads To Forest Supplies and Forestry*, Bulletin No. 1 (Washington, D.C.: GPO, 1887), 7; M. G. Kern, "The Relation Of Railroads To Forest Supplies and Forestry," in *Report On the Relation of Railroads To Forest Supplies and Forestry*, 13-23.

7. U.S. Department of Agriculture, Forestry Division, *Report On the Forest Conditions of the Rocky Mountains and Other Papers*, Bulletin No. 2 (Washington, D.C.: GPO, 1888), 7-13; E. A. James, "The Government In Its Relation To the Forests," in *Report On the Forest Conditions of the Rocky Mountains and Other Papers*, 26-27.

8. E. A. James, "The Government In Its Relation To the Forests," 30; Edward T. Ensign, "Report on the Forest Conditions of the Rocky Mountains, Especially in the State of Colorado, The Territories of Idaho, Montana, Wyoming, and New Mexico," in *Report On the Forest Conditions of the Rocky Mountains and Other Papers*, 100; ARSI 1888, XLVII.

9. J. P. Kinney, "The Administration of Indian Forests," *Journal of Forestry* 28:8 (December 1930): 1042; ARSI 1889, CXIV; "Report of the Surveyor-General of Montana," in ARSI 1890, 423; ARSI 1895, CXV.

10. "Synopsis of Report on Inspection of Flathead Agency by Inspector James Cisney," July 23, 1891, "Synopsis of Report on Inspection of Flathead Agency by Inspector McCormick," December 2, 1893, and "Report on Inspection of Flathead Agency by Inspector McCormick," February 18, 1895, NAmf M1070; Report of the Commissioner of the General Land Office," in ARSI 1897, 76-7.

11. ARSI 1898 in ARDI 1898, XIV; "Thinks Department Should interpose to prevent the consummation of an agreement for cession of west half of Flathead Reservation," Inspector W. J. McConnell to the Secretary of the Interior, August 27, 1897, NAmf M1070; ARCIA 1898, 191; ARCIA 1900, 52-3; ARCIA 1901, 49.

12. In 1903, the Interior Department combined the Lewis and Clarke and Flathead reserves under the former name. In 1906, the reserves included: Lewis and Clarke, Gallatin, Hell Gate, Little Belt Mountain, Madison, Highwood Mountains, Elkhorn, Big Belt, and Helena. ARSI 1906 in ARDI 1906, 553.

13. ARSI 1901 in ARDI 1901, 129; ARSI 1902 in ARDI 1902, 343; ARSI 1904 in ARDI 1904, 635.

14. *Timber, Tribes, and Trust*, 27-34; ARCIA 1906, 90-1; ARCIA 1908, 57; ARCIA 1909, 52.

15. *Timber, Tribes, and Trust*, 25; ARSI 1907 in ARDI 1907, 93; Commissioner Francis Leupp to United States Indian Agents, Circular 185, March 1908 and Acting Commissioner to United States Indian Agents, Circular 193, "Co-operative Plan relative to cutting and sale of timber," March 30, 1908, NAmf M1121-9.

16. C. H. Fitch, Acting Director, Reclamation Service, to H. N. Savage, Supervising Engineer, August 18, 1908, Box 62, Folder, "858. Funds, General, Flathead Project," GAF; Francis E. Leupp, Commissioner of Indian Affairs, to Senator Joseph M. Dixon, August 17, 1908, Box 7, Folder 4, "General Correspondence, August 21-24, 1908," JMD; Francis E. Leupp to Joseph M. Dixon, September 2, 1908, Box 7, Folder 6, "General Correspondence, September 1-9, 1908," JMD; Robert G. Valentine, Acting Commissioner of Indian Affairs, to Richard A. Ballinger, Secretary of the Interior, January 28, 1909, Philip P. Wells, Law Officer, U.S. Forest Service, "Memorandum for Mr. Woodruff," February 1, 1908, and Joseph M. Dixon, Senate Committee on the Conservation of National Resources, to Richard A. Ballinger, October 24, 1909, Box 1193, "5-1, Flathead, P-T," Folder, "Indian Office, Flathead, Timber. January 27, 1905-March 21, 1913," OS CCF.

17. Thomas E. Will, Secretary, American Forestry Association, to E. F. Tabor, Flathead Project Engineer, May 26, 1908 and Assistant Forester, U.S. Department of Agriculture, Forest Service, to E. F. Tabor, September 25, 1908, Box 2, Folder, "American Forestry Association," FIP GS; Gifford Pinchot, Chief Forester, U.S. Forest Service, to Montana Governor Edwin L. Norris, June 26, 1908 and William L. Hall, Acting Forester, U.S. Forest Service, to Edwin L. Norris, July 1, 1908, Box 172, Folder 2, "Agriculture-Conservation, 1908-1910," MGP; W. J. Cox, Assistant Forester, to Flathead Irrigation Project Engineer, August 27, 1908, Box 3, Folder, "Forest Service Matters Pertaining To," FIP GS.

18. E. F. Tabor, Flathead Project Engineer, to H. N. Savage, Supervising Engineer, Reclamation Service, August 26, 1908, Box 1, Folder, "Lumber," FIP GS; *Flathead Project, Montana: Annual Project History, 1910*, vol. 1, 10-11; Joseph M. Dixon to F. H. Newell, Director of the Reclamation Service, October 24, 1909, Box 473, Folder, "1004-B. Flathead, Repayments, Sale of Timber," GPF Joseph M. Dixon to R. A. Ballinger, Secretary of the Interior, October 24, 1909, Box 1193, "5-1, Flathead P-T," Folder, "Indian Office, Flathead, Timber. January 27, 1905-March 21, 1913," OS CCF.

19. "Pinchotism," *New York Post*, January 26, 1909 and "Pinchot and Ballinger," *Pittsburgh Dispatch*, July 26, 1909, Box 1, FHN; *Timber, Tribes, and Trust*, 34-6.

20. "Ballinger Clips Pinchot's Wings," *Chicago Tribune*, July 26, 1909, "Keep Newell In Office," *Chicago Post*, July 26, 1909, "Ballinger Has Way," *Washington Star*, July 26, 1909, and "Ballinger After Pinchot's Scalp," *Fresno Republican*, July 27, 1909, Box 1, FHN; *Timber, Tribes, and Trust*, 36; ARCIA 1912, 6; J. P. Kinney, *Indian Forest and Range: A History of the Administration and Conservation of the Redman's Heritage* (Washington, D.C.: Forestry Enterprises, 1950), 84-6.

21. James Penick, *Progressive Politics and Conservation: The Ballinger-Pinchot Affair* (Chicago: University of Chicago Press, 1968), ix-xiv, 181-96; Char Miller, *Gifford Pinchot and the Making of Modern Environmentalism* (Washington, D.C.: Island Press, 2001), 211, 353.

22. ARSI 1909 in ARDI 1909, 5; ARCIA 1909, 72; ARCIA 1912, 6.

23. An act of June 25, 1910, provided that sales of timber from tribal lands would be used for the benefit of the Indians rather than go into the Indian Office's general fund. Though no accurate records existed, the BIA estimated that prior to June of 1909 as much as two billion board feet had been taken from Indian lands across the United States. Some was taken through unlawful timber trespass and without compensation to the tribes, but much was cut through contracts set up by the BIA. Frequent allegations of government fraud were made about the funds gained from Indian timber. See J. P. Kinney, "The Administration of Indian Forests," 1043, 1048-49.

24. First Assistant Secretary to the Secretary of the Smithsonian Institution, May 25, 1910, Box 1188, "5-1, Flathead A-I," Folder, "Indian Office, Flathead, General. September 15, 1909-December 19, 1927," OS CCF; Fred Dennett, Commissioner of Indian Affairs, to F. H. Newell, Director of the Reclamation Service, January 28, 1910, Box 470, Folder, "1002. Flathead Project, Lands, General," GPF; "Annual Report of Fred C. Morgan on Flathead Agency, 1910," NAmf M1011-42.

25. Garret B. Holloway, "Golden Anniversary of Fiery Horror," *Montana, The Magazine of Western History* 10:4 (October, 1960): 49-54; ARCIA 1912, 6.

26. Secretary of Agriculture to R. A. Ballinger, Secretary of the Interior, October 22, 1910, C. F. Hauke, Acting Commissioner of Indian Affairs, to the Secretary of the Interior, November 7, 1910,

and R. A. Ballinger to the Secretary of Agriculture, November 8, 1910, Box 1193, "5-1, Flathead, P-T," Folder, "Indian Office, Flathead, Timber. January 27, 1905-March 21, 1913," OS CCF; A. P. Davis, Acting Director of the Reclamation Service, to H. N. Savage, Supervising Engineer, October 7, 1911, Box 262, Folder, "858. Funds, General, Indian Projects, Thru 1911," GAF; "Annual Report of Fred C. Morgan on Flathead Agency, 1911," NAmf M1011-42

27. ARSI 1910 in ARDI 1910, 112; *Timber, Tribes, and Trust*, 44; "Friends of the Flathead Will Try to Help Us," RP, April 5, 1912, 1.

28. The *Pioneer* concluded, "there is some timber on all such tracts, but the timber is worthless from a commercial standpoint...and good for nothing except for fuel." Some tracts did have fewer trees than others, but the blanket statement about all timbered lands lead to the real point: opening up this "best portion of the reservation" by removing the trees meant the success of non-Indian settlers by "the making of permanent and profitable homes." "Settlers Are Again Warned," RP, August 30, 1912, 1; "More About Timber Lands," RP, January 23, 1913, 1; Secretary of the Interior to the Attorney General, July 12, 1911, Box 1194, "5-1, Flathead T-W," Folder, "Indian Office, Flathead, Trespass – General," OS CCF.

29. Cato Sells, Commissioner of Indian Affairs, to the Secretary of the Interior, August 27, 1914, Box 1193, "5-1, Flathead, P-T," Folder, "Indian Office, Flathead, Timber. August 10, 1914-November 29, 1924," OS CCF; Secretary of the Interior to the Attorney General, July 12, 1911.

30. E. F. Tabor, Flathead Project Engineer, to H. N. Savage, Supervising Engineer, April 10. 1912, Box 469, Folder, "1001-1. Flathead Project, Miscellaneous Clippings," GPF; "Not Appraising the Reservation Lands Very Fast," RO, May 31, 1912, 1; Advertisement, Reservation Land and Lumber Company, Ronan, Montana, RP, February 16, 1912, 2; "Unappraised Lands Holding Back Improvements," RP, August 30, 1912, 4; *Flathead Annual Project History, 1912*, vol. 10, RG 115, 6, 43; ARCIA 1912, 220, 223.

31. ARCIA 1913, 2-3.

32. Records indicate the stumpage value of wood taken from tribal lands by all parties, but they do not indicate any exact figures of what contractors received when they sold the wood.

33. The Indian Office began employing the forest guards in 1911, one year after it disposed of the services of the U.S. Forest Service. "Annual Report of Fred C. Morgan on Flathead Agency, 1913" and "Annual Report of Fred C. Morgan on Flathead Agency, 1914," NAmf M1011-42; ARCIA 1913, 188, 191, 193; ARCIA 1914, 155, 158.

34. M. L. Dorr, "A Report to the Secretary of the Interior on the Flathead Indian Reservation," June 2, 1914, Box 1189, "5-1, Flathead I," no folder (loose in box), OS CCF.

35. "Annual Report of Fred C. Morgan on Flathead Agency, 1915," NAmf M1011-42; William H. Ketcham, *Report Upon the Conditions On the Flathead Reservation* (Washington, D.C.: Board of Indian Commissioners, 1915), 21-26; "Report of the Commissioner of the General Land Office," ARSI 1915 in ARDI 1915, 258.

36. Ketcham, 39, 42-3, 50, 61-2.

37. Ketcham, 62; "Report of the Commissioner of the General Land Office," ARSI 1915, 259; "Flathead Indian Guard Has An Unpopular Job," RP, November 26, 1915, 1.

38. ARSI 1915, 48.

39. "Annual Report of Fred C. Morgan on Flathead Agency, 1916," NAmf M1011-42; E. B. Meritt, Assistant Commissioner, to C. E. Dunston, Supervisor of Forests, July 31, 1916 and Cato Sells, Commissioner, to the Secretary of the Interior, April 28, 1917, Box 1193, "5-1, Flathead P-T," Folder, "Indian Office, Flathead, Timber. August 10, 1914-November 29, 1924," OS CCF; "Annual Report of Theodore Sharp on Flathead Agency, 1917," NAmf M1011-42

40. *Timber, Tribes, and Trust*, 62-3; "Annual Report of Theodore Sharp on Flathead Agency, 1917," NAmf M1011-42.

41. *Timber, Tribes, and Trust*, 51, 61-3; ARCIA 1917, 55; "Annual Report of Theodore Sharp on Flathead Agency, 1918," NAmf M1011-42.

42. J. P. Kinney, "Forest Policy on Indian Timberlands," *Journal of Forestry* 25:4 (April 1927): 431-32; ARSI 1918 in ARDI 1918, 59, 228-29; ARCIA 1918, 185.

43. "Annual Report of Theodore Sharp on Flathead Agency, 1919," NAmf M1011-42; ARCIA 1919, 173; "Flathead Indians Want To Run Own Affairs," RP, February 21, 1919, 1.

44. U.S. Congress, House, *Hearings Before the House Committee On Indian Affairs*, 66 Cong., 1st sess., as quoted in *Timber, Tribes, and Trust*, 36.

45. E. B. Meritt, Assistant Commissioner of Indian Affairs, to the Secretary of the Interior, April 17, 1919, Box 1193, "5-1, Flathead, P-T," Folder, "Indian Office, Flathead, Timber, August 10,

1914-November 29, 1924," OS CCF; "Annual Report of Charles E. Coe on Flathead Agency, 1920," NAmf M1011-42; Hugh L. Scott, "Report On the Flathead Indian Agency, Montana," in U.S. Board of Indian Commissioners, *Fifty-Second Annual Report of the Board of Indian Commissioners for the Fiscal Year Ended June 30, 1921* (Washington, D.C.: GOP, 1921), 64.

46. Cato Sells, Commissioner of Indian Affairs, to the Secretary of the Interior, May 8, 1920, Box 1193, "5-1, Flathead, P-T," Folder, "Indian Office, Flathead, Timber. August 10, 1914-November 29, 1924," OS CCF; "Annual Report of Charles E. Coe on Flathead Agency, 1920"; "Relief of Certain Members of the Flathead Nation of Indians," H.R. 545, 66th Cong., 2d sess., serial 7652 (Washington, D.C.: GPO, 1920), 2-3.

47. The Forest Service in the Department of Agriculture went as far as drawing up maps for the forests. J. P. Kinney argued that Agriculture employees hijacked the ideas set forth by Lane and did not even consult Indian Office foresters. Apparently, some BIA foresters, like Kinney, did not believe making Flathead and other Indian timberlands into national forests would be beneficial to the Indians. Though this created some disgruntlement between the Indian Office and Secretary Lane, a greater rift developed between Interior and Agriculture. See Kinney, *Indian Forest and Range*, 229-31.

48. The legislation also contained provisions for parceling out surplus tribal timberland as allotments to six hundred children who were born after the original period of allotment. In short, supervision of the timber on these lands would pass from Indian Office control to individual Indians. As Commissioner of Indian Affairs in the 1930s, John Collier would cite this provision as a major obstacle to conservation. ARCIA 1920, 52-3; "Relief of Certain Members of the Flathead Nation of Indians," 1-3.

49. ARCIA 1920, 108; ARCIA 1921, 30; "Annual Report of Charles E. Coe on Flathead Agency, 1922," NAmf M1011-42.

50. "Annual Report of Charles E. Coe on Flathead Agency, 1922"; "N.P. Is Sued For $236,766," RP, August 24, 1923, 1.

51. In 1924, the Polleys Lumber Company was the largest operator, cutting 18,230,280 feet at a value of $78,251.24 at its camps near Ronan. The Heron Lumber Company cut 8,428,720 feet at the Jocko camps with a valuation of $39,695.73 and 10,180,770 feet at a valuation of $32,076.64. The Dewey Lumber Company at Big Arm cut 5,281,400 feet worth $21,836.47. All the other operators cut 16,630,728 feet with a value of $52,247.22. "Four Million Feet Timber August Cut," RP, September 28, 1923, 1; ARSI 1923, 41; ARCIA 1923, 19; "Much Lumber Is Cut On Flathead," RP, January 30, 1925, 3.

52. "Annual Report of Charles E. Coe on Flathead Agency, 1925," NAmf M1011-43; "Coolidge Warns To Save Timber," RP, March 27, 1925, 3.

53. ARSI 1925, 6-8; J. P. Kinney, "The Administration of Indian Forests," 1044-45.

54. In that period, the timber cut on all Indian lands brought in over $16 million. ARCIA 1926, 21.

55. J. P. Kinney, "Forest Policy on Indian Timberlands," 430-35.

56. ARSI 1928, 72; *Extracts from the Annual Report of the Secretary of the Interior, 1928 Relating to the Bureau of Indian Affairs* (GPO, 1928), 71; ARCIA 1929, 12; *Timber, Tribes, and Trust*, 218-19; U.S. Senate, *Survey of Conditions of the Indians of the United States*, Part 31, "Montana," Hearings Before a Subcommittee of the Committee on Indian Affairs, 73rd Cong. (Washington, D.C.: GPO, 1934), 16779-16801.

57. ARCIA 1930, 17-8.

58. The Flathead were also likely opposed to grazing because drought struck Montana in 1919 and a severe winter followed in 1919-20. Unprepared for the climatic assault, the Flathead lost large amounts of livestock and then lack of grass required further reduction of herds. Thus, the Indians had reasonable apprehension about future grazing efforts. Charles D. Faunce and John W. Allan, "Working Plan Report of the Grazing Resources and Activities of the Flathead Indian Reservation, Montana," December 13, 1930, Box 5, Folder, "Working Plan Report of the Grazing Resources and Activities of the Flathead Indian Res., MT," BAO GC, 18, 32, 35-6, 39; Kinney, *Indian Forest and Range*, 254.

59. ARCIA 1932, 15-7.

60. John Collier, Ward Shepard, and Robert Marshall, "The Indians and Their Lands," *Journal of Forestry* 31:8 (December 1933): 907-08.

61. Ibid., 908-10.

62. Ibid., 910; Lee Muck to the Commissioner of Indian Affairs, September 27, 1934, Box 12, Folder 7, "Flathead, 1934-1935," MGO; Francis Paul Prucha, *The Great Father: The United States Government and the American Indians* (Lincoln: University of Nebraska Press, 1984, reprint, 1995), 985-87.

63. Lee Muck to the Commissioner of Indian Affairs, September 27, 1934; "The Indians and Their Lands," 907; "Administration of Indian Lands," S.R. 382, 73d Cong., 2d sess., serial 9769 (Washington, D.C.: GPO, 1934), 1-2.

64. Though the depression drastically reduced the amount of timber cut at Flathead, between one and one half and two and one half million feet of timber was cut per year for an income of about $5,000 to $10,000. *Survey of Conditions of the Indians of the United States*, Part 31, "Montana," 16777-167780.

65. "Statement of Charles E. Coe, Flathead Superintendent," and "Statement of Charles Faunce, Flathead Forest Supervisor," *Survey of Conditions of the Indians of the United States*, Part 31, "Montana," 16776-16780, 16805-07.

66. *Survey of Conditions of the Indians of the United States*, Part 31, "Montana," 16822, 16831-33.

67. Harold C. Brown, Forester, Flathead Reservation, to the Commissioner of Indian Affairs, February 1, 1935, Box 90, Folder, "18574-33," CCFF; John Collier, "A Birdseye View of Indian Policy: Historic and Contemporary," Submitted to the Sub-Committee of the Appropriation Committee of the House of Representatives, December 30, 1935, Box 1, Folder, "011. Publications–Indian Office," RG 75, Blackfeet Indian Agency, Blackfeet, Montana—Forestry and Grazing Correspondence, 1920-1950, Accession # 8NS-075-96-151 (National Archives, Denver), 12-3.

68. For instance, Superintendent Shotwell reported, "We have a curious situation. On the one hand, a Bureau of the Government [Biological Survey] is trying to protect birds through the establishment of bird refuges, and on the other hand, another division of the Government, the Irrigation Service, tears down the work as fast as it is accomplished.... Thousands of dollars are being spent to protect and propagate wild life and the Irrigation Service disregards all of these endeavors and destroys their efforts as fast as accomplished." L. W. Shotwell, Flathead Superintendent, to the Commissioner, June 5, 1936, Box 449, Folder, "29030, Flathead 1936," CCFF.

69. For more on the Mission Range Wilderness, see Diane L. Krahe, "A Sovereign Prescription for Preservation: The Mission Mountain Tribal Wilderness," in Richmond L. Clow and Imre Sutton, eds., *Trusteeship In Change: Toward Tribal Autonomy in Resource Management* (Boulder: University Press of Colorado, 2001), 195-224. L. W. Shotwell, Flathead Superintendent, to the Commissioner, June 5, 1936, Box 449, Folder, "29030, Flathead 1936," CCFF; John Collier, Commissioner of Indian Affairs, "Establishment of Roadless and Wild Areas On Indian Reservations," October 25, 1937, Box 105, Folder, "4852, Flathead 1938," CCFF.

70. L. W. Shotwell, Flathead Superintendent, to George M. Nyce, Regional Forester, August 20, 1938, George M. Nyce to the Commissioner of Indian Affairs, August 24, 1938, and W. C. Mendenhall, Assistant Secretary of the Interior, to the Comptroller of the United States, October 11, 1938, Box 9, Folder, "Flathead Indian Reservation, May 25, 1937 to November 16, 1939," BAO FRM.

71. L. W. Shotwell, Flathead Superintendent, to D. E. Murphy, Director, CCC-ID, June 28, 1938, L. W. Shotwell to the Commissioner of Indian Affairs, December 8, 1938, and L.W. Shotwell to the Commissioner of Indian Affairs, August 8, 1941, Box 90, Folder, "18574-33," CCC; George M. Nyce, Regional Forester, Indian Office, to the Commissioner of Indian Affairs, December 12, 1938 and George M. Nyce to the Commissioner of Indian Affairs, June 13, 1939, Box 9, Folder, "Flathead Indian Reservation, May 25, 1927-November 16, 1939," BAO FRM.

72. L. W. Shotwell, Flathead Superintendent, to D. E. Murphy, Director, CCC-ID, June 28, 1938, L. W. Shotwell to the Commissioner of Indian Affairs, October 26, 1938, and L. W. Shotwell to the Commissioner, May 19, 1939, Box 90, Folder, "18574-33," CCC; L. W. Shotwell to the Commissioner, October 21, 1938, Box 88, Folder, "50830-36, Funds," CCC.

73. This meant the annual cut could not exceed one percent of the total volume of merchantable timber on the reservation, ensuring a cutting rotation of 100 years. With an estimated 900 million feet of merchantable timber, this meant an annual cut of nine million feet, while the tribal charter enforced the replanting of clear-cut areas.

74. Director of Forestry, Indian Office, to George M. Nyce, Regional Forester, October 18, 1938, Box 9, Folder, "Flathead Indian Reservation, May 25, 1927-November 16, 1939," BAO FRM; "Testimony of S. C. De Mers, President, Tribal Council of Confederated Salish and Kootenai Tribes,"

U.S. House, *Investigate Indian Affairs*, Part 3, Hearings in the Field, Hearings Before a Subcommittee of the Committee on Indian Affairs, 78th Cong., 2d sess. (Washington, D.C.: GPO, 1945.), 452.

75. ARSI 1937, 209; *Timber, Tribes, and Trust*, 66; William Zimmerman, Assistant Commissioner, to Burton K. Wheeler, November 7, 1938 and U. S. Department of Agriculture, Soil Conservation Service, in cooperation with the BIA, "Reconnaissance Survey of the Flathead Indian Reservation, Montana," April, 1939, Box 9, Folder, "Flathead Indian Reservation, May 25, 1937 to November 16, 1939," BAO FRM; ARCIA 1938, 249.

76. *Timber, Tribes, and Trust*, 66; John Collier, Commissioner, to Superintendents and Forest Officers, August 25, 1941 and "Memorandum of Understanding Between the Fish and Wildlife Service and the Office of Indian Affairs," August 25, 1941, Box 449, Folder, "29030, Flathead 1936," CCFF.

77. L. W. Shotwell, Flathead Superintendent, to William Zimmerman, Assistant Commissioner, December 26, 1943, William Zimmerman to L. W. Shotwell, January 6, 1943, and L. W. Shotwell to the Commissioner, January 12, 1943, Box 449, Folder "77148, Flathead 1938," CCFF.

78. Testimony of S. C. DeMers, President, Tribal Council of Confederated Salish and Kootenai tribes and "Resolution of the Governing Body of the Confederated Salish and Kootenai Tribes of the Flathead Reservation," *Investigate Indian Affairs*, 452, 461.

79. "Statement of Albert Lemery," *Survey of Conditions of the Indians of the United States*, Part 31, "Montana," 16832; U.S. Department of Agriculture, Soil Conservation Service, in cooperation with the Bureau of Indian Affairs, "Reconnaissance Survey of the Flathead Indian Reservation, Montana," April, 1939, Box 9, Folder, "Flathead Indian Reservation, May 25, 1927-November 16, 1939," BAO FRM; F. H. Newell, "Irrigation of Indian Lands," An Address at the Lake Mohonk Conference on the Indian, Mohonk Lake, New York, October 15, 1929, Box 1435, "5-6, Insurance Irrigation," Folder, "Indian Office, General, Irrigation. August 2, 1919-April 7, 1930," OS CCF; *Timber, Tribes, and Trust*, 253.

80. Ralph G. Wiggenhorn, Attorney, to E. O. Fuller, August 3, 1951, Box 27, Folder, "General 4," EOF; E. O. Fuller, "Report: 1855 Land Values," September 30, 1953, Box 29, Folder, "Reports 5," EOF.

81. *Timber, Tribes, and Trust*, 218-219; John Collier, Ward Shepard, and Robert Marshall. "The Indians and Their Lands," 905; Gordon MacGregor, "The Social Aspects of the Economy of the Flathead Reservation," Office of Indian Education, 1939, page 20, Box 1, BAO FP; J. P. Kinney, Elwood R. Maunder, and George T. Morgan, "An Oral History Interview," *Forest History* 15 (July, 1971), 9, 12.

## Chapter 3

1. Charles D. Faunce and John W. Allan, "Working Plan Report of the Grazing Resources and Activities of the Flathead Indian Reservation, Montana," December 13, 1930, Box 5, Folder, "Working Plan Report of the Grazing Resources and Activities of the Flathead Indian Res., MT," BAO GC; Thomas E. Will, Secretary, American Forestry Association, to E. F. Tabor, May 26, 1908, Box 2, Folder, "American Forestry Association," FIP GS; W. J. Cox, Assistant Forester, to Flathead Irrigation Project Engineer, August 27, 1908, Box 3, Folder, "Forest Service Matters Pertaining To," FIP GS.

2. A. P. Davis, Acting Director, Reclamation Service, to R. A. Ballinger, Secretary of the Interior, April 10, 1909 and A. P. Davis, "Memorandum," April, 1909, Box 13, Folder 1, APDP; "Memorandum of Information: Flathead Irrigation Project," 1941, Box 13, Folder, "Flathead Crop Report, CY 1941," BAO MIA; "Pinchotism," *New York Post*, January 26, 1909, Box 1, FHN.

3. James Penick, *Progressive Politics and Conservation: The Ballinger-Pinchot Affair* (Chicago: University of Chicago Press, 1968), 47-59.

4. "Pinchot and Ballinger," *Pittsburgh Dispatch*, July 26, 1909 and "Ballinger After Pinchot's Scalp," *Fresno Republican*, July 27, 1909, Box 1, FHN; *Timber, Tribes, and Trust*, 35-6.

5. *Eighth Annual Report of the Reclamation Service, 1908-1909* (Washington, D.C.: GPO, 1910), 93; *Ninth Annual Report of the Reclamation Service, 1909-1910* (GPO, 1911), 144-45; *Flathead Project, Montana: Annual Project History, 1911*, RG 115, 68-70; ARCIA 1910, 21.

6. "Appraisement and Classification of Land Asked," RP, July 28, 1911, 1; Assistant Secretary of the Interior to the Attorney General, July 16, 1912 and Assistant Secretary of the Interior to

the Attorney General, October 30, 1913, Box 1194, "5-1, Flathead T-W," Folder, "Indian Office, Flathead, Trespass – General," OS CCF.

7. ARSI 1912 in ARDI 1912, 48; William H. Ketcham, *Report Upon the Conditions on the Flathead Indian Reservation* (Washington, D.C.: Board of Indian Commissioners, 1915), 18-21.

8. Frank Bailey to the Secretary of the Interior, April 30, 1913, Box 1189, "5-1, Flathead I," Folder, "Indian Office, Flathead, Irrigation, Fencing," OS CCF; Residents of the City of Polson, Montana, to the Secretary of the Interior, November 25, 1913 and F. H. Newell, "Memorandum for the Secretary," December 13, 1913, Box 1189, "5-1, Flathead I," Folder, "Indian Office, Flathead, Irrigation – Power Development," OS CCF.

9. Chief Engineer, Indian Irrigation Service, Memorandum, "Laws Pertaining to irrigation on the Flathead Reservation," January 29, 1914, Box 36, Folder, "Flathead Agency Files, 1910-1916," ID GC.

10. ARCIA 1914, 111; "Annual Report of Theodore Sharp on Flathead Agency, 1918" and "Annual Report of Theodore Sharp on Flathead Agency, 1919," NAmf M1011-42; ARSI 1919 in ARDI 1919, 261; Survey of Conditions, Part 10, 3386.

11. "Davis Out, Work To Davis To Work," *The Literary Digest*, July 21, 1923, Box 7, File, "Correspondence," GHE; A. P. Davis to Joseph Jacobs, July 5, 1923, Box 14, Folder 6, APDP.

12. A. P. Davis, "Memorandum," June 19, 1923, Box 14, Folder 7, APDP.

13. A. P. Davis to Joseph Jacobs, July 5, 1923; A. P. Davis to J. L. Lytel, July 25, 1923, Box 14, Folder 5, APDP; "Wanted: A Battle Cry," *New Mexico State Tribune*, July 11, 1923, page 4, Box 14, Folder 8, APDP.

14. "Wanted: A Battle Cry"; "Davis Out, Work To Davis To Work"; A. P. Davis to Hubert Work, June 19, 1923, Box 14, Folder 5, APDP; "Another Row Brewing," *Helena Independent*, July 7, 1923, Box 7, Folder, "Correspondence," GHE; A. P. Davis to Frank C. Wight, Editor, *Engineering News-Record*, July 18, 1924, Box 14, Folder 7, APDP.

15. "Regarding The Newell Tunnel," RP, March 6, 1925, 1, 4.

16. *Annual Report of the Board of Indian Commissioners, 1926* (GPO, 1926), 28; "Memorandum of Information: Flathead Irrigation Project," Box 13, Folder, "Flathead Crop Report, CY 1941," BAO MIA; C. C. Merrill, Secretary, Federal Power Commission, to Senator Thomas J. Walsh, February 3, 1926 and C. S. Heidel, Montana State Engineer, to J. E. Erickson, Governor of Montana, March 10, 1926, Box 181, Folder 1, "Flathead Power Project, 1922-1927," MPC.

17. Charles H. Burke to Senator Thomas J. Walsh, February 4, 1926 and C.S. Heidel to J. E. Erickson, March 10, 1926, Box 181, Folder 1, "Flathead Power Project, 1922-1927," MPC; "Flathead Counsel Will Fight Power Dam Construction," RP, July 16, 1926, 1.

18. The government had spent over $100,000 on the Newell Tunnel but basically abandoned further development because it did not seem "a wise investment nor an economic way of getting the water on the land." Moreover, federal officials delayed the project because the Flathead region of Montana remained relatively undeveloped. In 1926, the $395,000 appropriated by congress renewed power plans, but then in 1927 the body decided private development would prove more feasible. "House Gives Montana Power Rights On Flathead Project," *Great Falls Tribune*, February 27, 1927, Box 5, Folder, "Flathead Development," CTM; "Irrigation Systems, Flathead Reservation, Mont.," H. Doc. 757, 69th Cong., 2d sess., serial 8735 (Washington, D.C.: GPO, 1927), 2-3.

19. Thomas J. Walsh, "Address at Ronan," August 3, 1927, Box 1190, "5-1, Flathead I," Folder, "Indian Office, Flathead, Irrigation – Power Development. January 25, 1924-January 11, 1930," OS CCF.

20. Ibid.

21. "Indian Power Right Sale Is Delayed," *Washington* (D.C.) *News*, September 9, 1927, Box 530, Folder, "320. Flathead Project, Correspondence re. Development of Power," GPF; A. A. Grorud, Attorney for Flathead Tribal Council, to Burton K. Wheeler, October 17, 1927 and J. W. Anderson, Secretary to Burton K. Wheeler, to Hubert Work, Secretary of the Interior, October 18, 1927, Box 1190, "5-1, Flathead I," Folder, "Indian Office, Flathead, Irrigation – Power Development. January 25, 1924-January 11, 1930," OS CCF.

22. Thomas J. Walsh, "Address at Ronan"; Survey of Conditions, Part 10, 3394-95, 3418-21.

23. R. A. Moncrieff, Consulting Engineer, Charles T. Main, Inc., to W. F. Uhl, May 23, 1928, Box 5, Folder, "Flathead Development," CTM; *Extracts from the Annual Report of the Secretary of the Interior, 1928 Relating to the Bureau of Indian Affairs* (GPO, 1928), 73; Survey of Conditions, Part 10, 42-3.

24. A. P. Davis to Joseph Jacobs, July 5, 1923; Frank Scotten, Manager, Montana Power Company, to Charles W. Helmrick, Helena, Montana, August 29, 1927, Box 181, Folder 1, "Flathead Power Project, 1922-1927," MPC; A. F. Walter, Chief Engineer, Reclamation Service, to Elwood Mead, Commissioner of the Reclamation Service, October 18, 1929, Box 530, Folder, "320. Flathead Project, Correspondence re. Development of Power," PF.

25. "Annual Report of Charles E. Coe on Flathead Agency, 1929," NAmf M1011-43; Survey of Conditions, Part 10, 3295.

26. The Federal Power Commission hearings lasted close to two weeks in October and November of 1929. They were the most "exhaustive" hearings ever held in a power site case." "The Flathead Power Case," *Washington* (D.C.) *News*, October 24, 1929, "Investigation Asked Into Plans to Develop Flathead Power Site," *U.S. Daily*, November 1, 1929, and "Power Company Asks That Profit Shares Be Denied Indians," *U.S. Daily*, November 8, 1929, Box 530, Folder, "320. Flathead Project, Correspondence re. Development of Power," PF; Survey of Conditions, Part 10, 3387-88.

27. American Indian Defense Association to Scott Leavitt, Chairman, House Committee on Indian Affairs, December 12, 1929, Box 940, Folder, "38841-1920," CCF; "To Develop Power and Lease, For Power Purposes, Structures of Indian Irrigation Projects," H.R. 2062, 70th Cong., 2d sess., serial 8979 (Washington, D.C.: GPO, 1929), 1-2; Michael P. Malone, "An Interview With Senator Burton K. Wheeler," May 23, 1970, Box 3, Folder 15, "Michael P. Malone Interview of Burton K. Wheeler, 1970," Burton K. Wheeler Papers, Collection 2207 (Merrill G. Burlingame Special Collections, Montana State University, Bozeman, Montana).

28. Survey of Conditions, Part 10, 3289-90, 3388.

29. Ibid., 3289-90, 3506; "Annual Report of Charles E. Coe on Flathead Agency, 1930," NAmf M1011-43; Caville Dupuis, President, Flathead Tribal Council, to Lynn J. Frazier, Chairman, Senate Committee on Indian Affairs, February 15, 1930, Box 1190, "5-1, Flathead I," Folder, "Indian Office, Flathead, Irrigation–Power Development. January 16, 1930-May 24, 1930," OS CCF; John Collier, "Monopoly In Montana," *The New Freeman* 1:8 (May 3, 1930): 178-80.

30. "Monopoly In Montana"; "An Old American Custom," *The New Freeman* 1:8 (May 3, 1930): 175-76; John Collier, "The Flathead Water-Power Lease," *The New Republic* 64:820 (August 20, 1930): 20-21.

31. Congress wanted to avoid another Muscle Shoals debacle, which was a drawn-out political struggle that contributed to a failure to promptly get anyone contracted to buy the power. Survey of Conditions, Part 10, 3382, 3386, 3389-90, 3494-95; "Flathead Power Development," S. Doc. 153, 71st Cong., 2d sess., serial 9220 (Washington, D.C.: GPO, 1930), 2-3, 16.

32. Survey of Conditions, Part 10, 3392-93, 3401.

33. Ibid., 3389, 3393, 3403, 3408-09, 3414-15, 3432-35, 3440; "Monopoly In Montana," 179-80.

34. The Montana Power Company argued that the revenue to the Indians should be determined by the amount of acreage they had in relation to the total storage area. The War Department adopted this "perfectly ridiculous" proposition as a means of determining what revenue the Indians should get.

35. Survey of Conditions, Part 10, 3470, 3475-83.

36. Ibid., 3428-30, 3477, 3510-11; "Flathead Power Development,"4-6, 42.

37. Under the license and upon completion of construction, slated for 1934, the Flathead would receive royalties ranging from $60,000 per year for the first two calendar years after the completion of construction to the sum of $175,000 per year from the third to the 16th year. "Flathead Power Development,"42-3; ARSI 1930, 31; ARCIA 1930, 24; Burton K. Wheeler, *Yankee From the West: The Candid, Turbulent Life Story of the Yankee-Born U.S. Senator From Montana* (Garden City, New York: Doubleday & Company, Inc., 1962), 315-16.

38. "Annual Report of Charles E. Coe on Flathead Agency, 1931," NAmf M1011-43; ARCIA 1931, 19; J. Henry Scattergood, Assistant Commissioner, "Memorandum for the Secretary of the Interior," September 15, 1932 and J. Henry Scattergood, "Memorandum for Secretary Wilbur," March 2, 1933, Box 1190, "5-1, Flathead I," Folder, "Indian Office, Flathead, Irrigation – Power Development. September 30, 1932-December 28, 1936," OS CCF.

39. Commissioners of the Mission Irrigation District to the Secretary of the Interior, October 30, 1933, in U.S. Senate, *Survey of Conditions of the Indians of the United States*, Part 31, "Montana," Hearings Before a Subcommittee of the Committee on Indian Affairs, 73rd Cong. (Washington, D.C.: GPO, 1934), 16871-74; John Collier, Commissioner, to Burton K. Wheeler, March 7, 1934 and Harold L. Ickes, Secretary of the Interior, to Frank R. McNinch, Chairman, Federal Power Commission, August 16, 1934, Box 1190, "5-1, Flathead I," Folder, "Indian Office, Flathead, Irrigation – Power Development. September 30, 1932-December 28, 1936," OS CCF; "The Development and Leasing of the Flathead Power Sites, Flathead Indian Reservation, Mont.," S.R. 147, 73d Cong., 2d sess., serial 9772 (Washington, D.C.: GPO, 1934), 1-2.

40. Harold L. Ickes to the Attorney General, January 2, 1936, Frederic L. Kirgis, Acting Solicitor of the Interior, "Memorandum for the Secretary," June 5, 1936, and Harold L. Ickes to Edwin Dupuis, President, Confederated Salish and Kootenai Tribal Council, June 30, 1936, Box 1190, "5-1, Flathead I," Folder, "Indian Office, Flathead, Irrigation – Power Development. September 30, 1932-December 28, 1936," OS CCF; ARCIA 1936 in ARSI 1936, 200-01.

41. ARSI 1933, 90; "Flathead Irrigation Project: Annual Irrigation Cost and Narrative Reports for Fiscal Year 1937," Box 13, Folder, "Flathead Annual Reports, 1937," "Flathead Irrigation Project: Annual Irrigation Cost and Narrative Reports for Fiscal Year 1938," Box 13, Folder, "Flathead Annual Reports, 1938," "Flathead Irrigation Project: Annual Irrigation Cost and Narrative Reports for Fiscal Year 1939," Box 13, Folder, "Flathead Annual Reports, 1939," and "Monthly Report for June 1940," Box 13, Folder, "Flathead Project Power System Monthly Reports, FY 1940," BAO MIA; William Zimmerman, Assistant Commissioner, to Burton K. Wheeler, November 7, 1938, Box 9, Folder, "Flathead Indian Reservation, May 25, 1937 to November 16, 1939," BAO FRM.

42. John Collier, Commissioner of Indian Affairs, to the Secretary of the Interior, July 1, 1942 and W. S. Hanna, District Engineer, Indian Irrigation Service, to C. H. Southworth, Acting Director of Irrigation, July 31, 1942, Box 13, Folder, "U.S. I.I.S, Flathead 1942," BAO MIA.

43. John Collier to the Secretary of the Interior, July 1, 1942; H. H. Cochrane, Montana Power Company, to Kenneth R. L. Simmons, District Counsel, Indian Office, July 17, 1942 and G. L. Sperry, Flathead Project Engineer, to Montana Power Company, July 21, 1942, Box 13, Folder, "U.S. I.I.S, Flathead 1942," BAO MIA; W. S. Hanna to C. H. Southworth, July 31, 1942; C. C. Wright, Superintendent, "General Information About the Flathead Indian Reservation in Western Montana," May 16, 1945, Walter Stanley Campbell (Stanley Vestal) Collection, Box 118, Folder 11 (Western History Collections, University of Oklahoma Libraries).

44. Barry Dibble, Consulting Engineer to the Tribes, to R. W. Lincoln, May 14, 1957 and John W. Cragun to Barry Dibble, May 28, 1957, Box 1, Folder, "Correspondence, 1957-1959," RWL; R. Wayne Lincoln, "Determination Of Indian Rentals For the Third Unit At Kerr Project – Montana," June 21, 1958 and Ralph A. Tudor, Consulting Engineer, to Joseph A. McElwain, September 10, 1958, Box 1, Folder, "Flathead Project," RWL; John W. Cragun, Attorney for the Flathead Tribe, to the Montana Congressional Delegation, September 19, 1958, Box 2, Folder, "Flathead Project Hearing, 1958," RWL.

45. *The Montana Power Company v. Federal Power Commission*, "Petition For Review Of An Order Of the Federal Power Commission," December 1959, Box 1, Folder, "Flathead Project," RWL; Walter W. McDonald and Robert A. McCree, Confederated Salish and Kootenai Tribal Council, "Resolution NO. 1062," November 3, 1959, Box 2, Folder, "Kerr Project, Montana," RWL; The Confederated Salish and Kootenai Tribes, "Background of the Problem of the Indians of the Flathead Reservation and Their Dam Sites," May 2, 1960, page 1, Box 2, Folder, "Montana Power Company, John Cragun Papers," RWL.

46. In 1960, because of the Corps of Engineers' plans for developing the Knowles dam, the Flathead could not convince Montana Power to develop tribal power site number two and number four, known as "Buffalo Rapids."

47. "Background of the Problem of the Indians of the Flathead Reservation and Their Dam Sites," pages 2-11.

48. John W. Cragun to the Confederated Salish and Kootenai Tribal Council, September 1, 1961 and John W. Cragun, "Brief of Intervenor [Confederated Tribes]," *The Montana Power Company v. The Federal Power Commission*, United States Court of Appeals, District of Columbia, September 1, 1961, Box 2, Folder, "Montana Power Company, John Cragun Papers," RWL; *Yankee From the West*, 316.

49. From 1960 to the early 1980s, tribal revenue from power did increase, but not in a manner commensurate with the rising market value of power. Jaako Puisto, "'This Is My Reservation, I Belong Here': The Salish Kootenai Struggle Against Termination" (Ph.D. Dissertation, Arizona State University, 2000), 75; D'Arcy McNickle, *Wind From An Enemy Sky* (Albuquerque: University of New Mexico Press, 1978), 1-2, 9.

50. James J. Lopach, Margaret Hunter Brown, and Richmond L. Clow, *Tribal Government Today: Politics on Montana Indian Reservations* (Niwot: University Press of Colorado, 1990), 178, 182-3; Dillon Kato, "CSKT Officially Assumes Ownership of Kerr Dam, Announces New Name," *The Missoulian*, September 5, 2015.

51. James David Bruggers "Natural Resources, Economic Development And Self-Determination On Montana's Indian Reservations: The Salish And Kootenai Example" (Master's thesis, University of Montana, 1987), 16-17; Joseph Kinsey Howard, "The Decline and Fall of Burton K. Wheeler," in Michael P. Malone and Richard B. Roeder, *The Montana Past: An Anthology* (Missoula: University of Montana Press, 1969), 284.

# Index

## The Author

Garrit Voggesser is the National Director of the National Wildlife Federation's Tribal Partnerships Program. Voggesser works with tribes across the nation on wildlife and habitat conservation, water policy and riparian restoration, energy and climate issues impacting tribes, and youth environmental education. Since 2004, Voggesser has led NWF's conservation partnership efforts with tribes. He received his doctorate in Native American and environmental history from the University of Oklahoma.